A Lock-Crete

CU00409670

Elise Williams

Written in the Lockdown of 2020

For Mitera mou - my mother

To love Greece you have to embrace rather than despair at the chaos that is the beauty that lives cheek by jowl with dereliction

A Lock up on Crete

A Lock up on Crete

A Lock up on Crete

Part 1

Chapter 1

<u>Zoe Matthews</u>
<u>Guernsey, Channel Islands, October 1984</u>
I did it! He's gone – departed the island on the overnight ferry back to the mainland. The port and brandy soothes my mixed emotions. I am free again. Free from his incessant gambling. My hard earned money belongs to me again. I don't know where I'll go from here but what I do know, is that it will be in the right direction.

<u>Melissa Longthorn</u>
<u>Guernsey, October 1984</u>
I did it! I've posted the letter. I didn't have the heart to phone Tom and tell him I'm not coming back for the winter. I will miss my hometown but I know it will bring back all the horror of the hit and run. I will return one

day but for now, the magnetic island of Crete will hopefully soothe my aching heart.

Tia Russo
Guernsey, October 1984
I did it! I phoned him last night to confirm that our 'two month rest period' has well and truly rested and the next period of my life will be without him. These two months in the idyllic island of Guernsey have taught me that there is more to life than waiting for him like a faithful puppy to return from his stint on the oil rigs.
There was a long pause before he spoke as I thought about the consequences of my actions and how it would dent his pride and narcissistic ways. Admittedly, he was the epitome of a Greek Adonis, with his smouldering looks but as I've found out the hard way, looks are deceptive. I am now free; free from his shackles; free to do whatever I want, when I want.

Agios Nikolaos, East Crete, October 1984

The cosmopolitan town of Agios Nikolaos was reluctantly drawing its summer season to a close. The tradesmen had already entered town, armed with plaster, paint and a plethora of white plastic buckets.

Old Manolis Mariakis sat outside his kafenion, ruminating whether this season should be his last before handing his forty year old business, to his only surviving family member, his nephew Andreas.

A Lock up on Crete

On the other side of the pretty harbour, Apollonia folded the last of the day's service wash and waited for its owner. She lived in a small room above the laundrette which she had managed for the last thirty years as a spinster. A chill came rushing in the room, reminding her that summer was now a distant memory, along with all the holiday makers. Apollonia wrapped the black shawl around her thin shoulders as she spotted three young women walking down the hill from the bus station. Two wore large backpacks while the other young woman struggled with a cumbersome suitcase, as it reluctantly trailed behind her like a moping teenager. Apollonia prided herself, despite her advancing years, for having a good sense of the female species that frequented her town. These three young women were definitely British, she concluded. Somehow she felt they might be trouble but if they kept away from her patch then nobody would come to any harm. She followed the girls with sharp, beady eyes as they searched the narrow street for their lodgings.

Two of the young women had the typical English rose complexions, one having bright curly red hair tamed into a bobble on top of her head, the other a neat, dark bob. The third had an almost southern Mediterranean complexion with a choice of attire which seemed too formal compared to her friends. Apollonia chuckled to herself as the red head irritably swapped her backpack and snatched the posh one's suitcase to navigate the steps up to the small hotel where she herself would be starting her other cleaning job soon when the last

A Lock up on Crete

person had collected their service wash. She might even be able to eavesdrop if she lingered outside their room. As it was out of season, Apollonia was intrigued as to what brought these three girls to her town. They were too late if they wanted to party; the majority of the bars and clubs, which catered for the pretty European girls and the Greek kamakis, had already shut up shop for the season.

'Tia, why on earth did you bring this bloody big suitcase with you?' Mel huffed as they eventually fell onto their narrow beds in the three bedded room.
'What do you mean? We're here for winter as well so I had to bring two sets of clothes. Besides, my mum is sending me more when we get an address,' Tia explained as she tore a plaster open and threw her court shoes under her bed.
Zoe winced at the huge blister that had formed on Tia's heel as she pulled back the heavy curtains, allowing a beam of light to enter the dimly lit room.
'Come on, let's go for a beer, it's been a long day,' Zoe suggested as she opened the door to find a thin, older woman scuttle away into a cleaning cupboard along the corridor.

The three English 'touristees' walked single file down the narrow pavement to the small town beach, as dozens of pairs of eyes watched from shop fronts and balconies. They took their seats looking seaward and ordered three large beers at the first bar they came to.

A Lock up on Crete

'Does anyone else get the feeling we are being watched?' Tia asked as she looked from left to right. 'Don't worry it's just the Cretan way. It's because we've just arrived in town when all the other tourists have left. They probably wonder what we are here for to be honest,' explained Mel, reminiscing on her first time to the island of Crete, some four years previously.

Mel, the redheaded girl had been relieved and excited, when, over a boozy night at the Seaview Hotel in Guernsey, where all three girls had met, that Zoe and Tia were both contemplating where to go next as the season drew to a close. A week later they were all relieved they had remembered their drunken and animated conversation and their plans to travel to Crete for the winter were still very much real.

As the late October sun descended and cast a beautiful pink hue over the mountains to the East, the three friends paid their bill and swayed in single file back up to the harbour front. Zoe insisted they must have something to eat before they retired for the night, ready for their busy day in the morning.

'Sorry but I think we should start as we mean to go on and eat where the locals eat. We can't afford to eat like tourists if we want to stay the whole winter,' suggested Mel as Tia paused to peruse the tourist menus where the aroma of herbs and garlic swirled in the gentle evening breeze. Reluctantly, she shook her head to the smiling waiter and followed her friends across the road and up the hill.

A Lock up on Crete

Meanwhile, old Manolis Mariakis was about to close for the night as the three girls sauntered into his kafenion. He was relieved that old Costas and Nikos had just left and the kafenion was empty or he might have been in for a long night. Within ten minutes, he had managed to rustle up a hearty meal for the girls, accompanied by half a carafe of Raki, a clear and fragrant liquor.

'You drink Raki. It is how we express our Cretan hospitality. It will make you sleep well,' Manolis explained as he poured the clear liquid into four shot glasses.

'Yamas,' he said as they all downed it in one.

'Arghhh! What the hell do they make that Raki with? My bloody head is banging on my brain!' Zoe moaned into her pillow the next morning. Tia slept soundly with her eye mask on as Mel supressed a giggle.

'That's not the first and last time you'll feel like this and remember you can't refuse a Cretan host their offer of Raki. No doubt it will be their own family produce,' Mel explained as her friend sighed and turned over in the narrow bed.

Outside their room, Apollonia strained her ears to hear. She prided herself, despite her advancing years, of how she had persevered and picked up snippets of English and could conduct a lengthy conversation with the foreign seasonal workers who would come in to the launderette with their bundles of stinking clothing. She was annoyed however, that the doors were so solid that all she could hear was a lot of moaning and groaning. When they eventually went out she would clean the

A Lock up on Crete

room and have a good look at their belongings. There must be a clue somewhere in the room as to what their intentions were, she told herself.

Iraepetra, South Crete

On the bus to Iraepetra, a few days later, it soon became clear to Zoe and Tia that any ideas they had of enjoying the last of the autumn sunshine would not be on the agenda as Mel explained how the southern agricultural town, renowned for its rolling white sea of greenhouses, needed foreign workers to tend to their abundant crops. 'There was plenty of work around when I was here four years ago and hopefully the locals will remember me,' Mel added as Tia stared out of the window, wondering where all the tourist shops and chic restaurants were. A few minutes later the bus arrived at its destination.

In the launderette, adjacent to the small bus station , Apollonia, covering a member of staff who had fallen ill, struggled to reach the high machine. She was exhausted after the early start to catch the first bus from Agios Nikolaos to Ireapetra, an hour's journey, in time to open up. Balancing on the rickety wooden stool she hauled a wash load into the machine as she caught a glimpse of three young women marching past the window. She shook her head, wondering if she was seeing things as her low blood pressure often made her dizzy and a little confused.

Plonking themselves down on the cushioned seats outside the first café bar, Tia toddled off to the loo while Mel ventured inside to check the staff and order some drinks. It was a matter of seconds before the barman yelled out Mel's name and threw his arms round her and swept up her red curls and twirled them around his fingers like a corkscrew. Maybe a past conquest, Zoe thought to herself as she continued to look through her Greek phrase book for 'absolute beginners.'

Zoe felt eyes upon her as she continued flicking through the pages, trying to decipher the strange looking Greek letters. Suddenly a coin dropped by her feet.

'Hello. Are you girls looking for somewhere to stay?' a rather good looking male asked as Zoe picked the coin up and handed it back, trying her best not to appear too naïve and needy.

'My friend is sorting our accommodation thanks,' Zoe replied just as Mel sauntered out again with the drinks and a plateful of snacks.

'Ahhh Damianos if I remember rightly,' Mel said to the good looking male as he stood up to greet her.

'Ahhh yes you do have a good memory Mel. It's good to see you. Are you back for good this time?' he enquired as Tia emerged from the toilets with her nose screwed up.

'Oh my good God in heaven above! I hope that toilet is just a one off. It absolutely reeks in there and some disgusting people have not bothered to put the loo roll down the loo.'

Zoe and Mel looked at each other realising that Tia must have drifted off to sleep in their rented room in Agios Nikolaos when Mel had explained about the Greek toileting system.

A Lock up on Crete

Mel turned to Damianos with folded arms.

'So Damianos. What are you up to these days apart from chatting up my friend?'

'I know a good apartment that's much cheaper than this one,' Damianos said looking up to the rooms for rent overlooking the sea.

It was as if he had hypnotised them, as no sooner had they paid their bill, they were following him a couple of hundred metres to a smart apartment block. They were greeted by a smartly dressed man who introduced himself as Theo. In a matter of minutes they had chosen their three bedded apartment, agreed on a long term rental price and returned to the foyer where Damianos scribbled in a small notepad.

'It is a good price you have agreed on and Theo is a good landlord,' Damianos said as he tore off a piece of paper and handed it to Zoe.

He bid them farewell as the girls collected their baggage and made their way up the stairs to their new home. Zoe discreetly opened the paper. *Meet me tonight at the Oasis bar —bring your girlfriends.*

'How did Damianos know how much rent we had agreed on with Theo anyway?' Tia asked as they familiarised themselves with the compact kitchen and made their first brew.

'I don't know but he's invited us to the Oasis bar tonight if you feel up to it?' Zoe revealed as she struggled with her emotions: either these Cretan men were rather forward and it was just their way or Damianos was not to be trusted. Unfortunately, Mel couldn't shed any light on him either. She had met him only a couple of times through her friend Yannis, four years previously.

An hour later, despite their intentions to have a few drinks in town, after a quick visit to a gyros stall, just around the corner from the apartment, the girls crawled into their respective beds, waking at noon the next day to an almighty hammering on their door. Mel wearily dragged her weary body to the door as Theo placed three heavy, brown blankets into her arms.

'You will need these soon. It can get cold soon. The rent is due on the 16 of each month,' Theo peered behind Mel into the apartment.

'Who was that?' Zoe enquired as she lifted her head from the depths of the pillow.

'It's ok, just our new landlord,' Mel reassured as she wondered if Theo had been given a personality transplant since the day before; his wide smile had somehow morphed into a thin sneer.

'Bloody inconsiderate of him at this early hour,' muttered Zoe as she returned to her crisp white pillow.

Chapter 2

Back in Agios Nikolaos, Old Manolis Mariakis searched through his receipts from the night the three touristee girls had eaten at his kafenion. He needed to find them fast. He held in his hand a fake 10,000 drachma note and he was absolutely certain the red haired touristee woman had paid the bill with it. He must find her in case

A Lock up on Crete

she had a stash full with the intention of tricking the older business people like himself with them. Old Manolis had always prided himself on his business astuteness and was feeling very cheated as he sipped his morning frappe, securing the fake note in an envelope to take to his cousin who manned the desk at the police station. Like Apollonia, he too wondered why the three touristees had just arrived as the season was closing. He thought back to the young voluptuous Apollonia and the way she swayed her hips – if only she had been more accommodating.

Meanwhile, Apollonia struggled even more than usual as she stepped down from the morning bus from Iraepetra. The two day cover at the launderette in Iraepetra had really taken its toll with the taller machines and a much heavier workload. She was relieved Rhea had made a speedy recovery and had returned to the launderette the evening before allowing Apollonia to return to her own launderette. Despite being born in Iraepetra, Apollonia had adopted Agios Nikolaos as her real home and her patch where she could exert control.

'Kalimera Manolis,' Apollonia hailed as she caught sight of him sat outside his kafenion on the descent into the town centre. He'd been a permanent fixture for time immemorial she reflected as she smiled at the memory of when he had shyly asked her out on a date, not realising he'd been beaten to it only an hour beforehand by the stylish Stelios. And as far as Apollonia knew, he had never married but then again, nor had she! She

A Lock up on Crete

could easily have had Stelios but had discovered he was from a poor family so had ended their courtship.

Manolis sprang to his feet and stepped into the road stopping the traffic to allow her to cross.

'Apollonia, Apollonia, Ela, Ela. You look exhausted. Where have you been?'

'What's wrong?' she asked as Manolis clacked his kolomboli worry beads with more force than usual.

'I've been robbed Apollonia. Three new touristees, a few nights ago. I was so tired yet I made them a hearty meal. Damn them Apollonia, Damn them!'

Apollonia drew her hand to her chest.

'Manolis, I have seen them too. Three English women. They are trouble I fear.' She cast her weary mind back to the launderette in Iraepetra. 'Manolis I will find them for you. I should trust my instincts more. I knew when I first set my eyes upon them. Leave it to me Manolis. I will hunt them down.'

For the first time in months, Apollonia felt a new wave of energy. Instinctively, she planted a kiss on Manolis' cheek and skipped down to the harbour where her only friend, Elpida, had been looking after her launderette.

In Iraepetra, Zoe struggled sleeping. She couldn't quite get the image of Damianos out of her head. How on earth could these Greek males be so beautiful she asked herself at 4 am in the morning. Just hours ago in town, she had spotted Damianos with a beautiful blonde girl in the corner of the last bar. She had felt a pang of envy as the girl slipped her hand through his. Mel had been at the bar ordering their last drinks and reminiscing with the bar staff while Tia had reluctantly needed to go to the loo. Zoe felt very awkward and could bear it no longer as she went in search of Tia, who had been gone far too long.

'Oh, Tia. I was wondering where you were,' Zoe swung the saloon- style door a little too hard to find Tia and a tall, blond man gazing at each other amid the putrid stench of the nearby loo, both totally oblivious she was there. Slinking back to her seat in the bar, Zoe was relieved to find that Damianos and his girl had gone as she accepted Metaxa brandy from Mel.

Kalimera – good morning
Tia

The October sun pierced the crack in the heavy curtains like a laser beam and a cacophony of sounds rose from the busy streets below. Tia woke with a start, wondering if her recent dream was indeed real. She glanced around at the dazzling white plastered walls to see Mel's hair spread out like red spirals on her pillow and Zoe's usually neat bobbed hair, spread like a tangled dark mop. She quickly made sure she was in her bed on her own as warm thoughts of Andreas soothed the fuzziness in her head. While Zoe and Mel slept, her thoughts returned to her hometown, a gritty, working town between Glasgow and Edinburgh. She could just imagine the scene last night at the local social club. She imagined how Chris would have handled her departure and the excuses he would have come up with, surrounding her absence. Of course, the majority of the social club knew exactly why she had broken up with him and most of the locals

A Lock up on Crete

would probably be appeasing him despite them really wanting to say what a 'self-centered loser' he was. But they knew from past experience how difficult it was for a narcissist to accept the way others perceived them. With or without good looks, it really didn't mean a damned thing when people can see right through you, especially your ex fiancé. Although Tia was now another world away and really not in the slightest bit interested in Chris, she reminded herself to phone her sister later that day just for an update. Until then, she would lay back and dream of Andreas. A smile crept on her face as she recalled how ironic it had been, given her distaste for Greek toilets that their eyes had met and riveted them both to the spot outside the putrid loos.

Mel

Mel struggled to come round: her head felt like a huge balloon. Far too many shots of the addictive Metaxa last night had certainly written a morning stroll on the beach off. She honestly didn't think that so many people had remembered her from her last visit four years ago. Even Maria, the older lady from the café bar where she had worked for a while making toasties, had peeped up to say hello from the serving hatch. It was nice to see that Maria was still going strong and probably much younger than her black widow weeds suggested. A new wave of euphoria and belonging swept over Mel since she'd returned to Crete. Working in Guernsey for the summer had helped her grieve her friend's sudden death in a hit and run but returning to Crete was the soothing arms she had yearned for. And, although she missed her crazy

A Lock up on Crete

girlfriends back home and her work at the Moorhouse restaurant where she had acquired her baking skills, she knew she had made the right decision to return to Crete. Tom, the owner of the restaurant was disappointed she wasn't going back to spoil everyone with her pastry skills but had wished her luck all the same. She did miss turning raw ingredients into the most amazing cake and pastry creations, but she knew her skills would never leave her and she could return to the industry at any time. She also remembered the raucous she had started at the village summer fete when her Victoria sponge had won first place; the shock on the face of Doris the Women's Institute treasurer, who had kept hold of the title for the century in succession was priceless. Mel drifted back off back to sleep with a smile upon her face and utter contentment in her heart.

Zoe

Zoe stirred, glad that she had chosen the bed next to the balcony, as a warm October breeze swirled in through the gap in the balcony doors and caressed her face. She glanced around her new abode, pleased to see that they had all made it back last night and the other two were soundly asleep. She carefully lifted her head from the soft pillow in an attempt to go to the loo, but her body refused. Her mind drifted back to her thoughts about Damianos and then onto Rick, her ex – she wondered what he was up to back on the mainland - probably gambling to his heart's content and living off beans and noodles. She couldn't believe she had put up with his errant ways for so long and knew there wasn't even an inch in her heart or mind that he now occupied. She had no regrets whatsoever, especially with all these gorgeous Greek males to admire all day, every day!

Chapter 3

Work calls!
After a few days lounging about and taking advantage of the mini October heatwave, the three girls knew they had to act on the job connections that Mel had been tirelessly securing for them. Sat outside Fotis's café bar, while Mel liaised with their future employers, Tia and Zoe took the chance to delve into each other's lives. They chatted about their families back home, ex boyfriends and their dreams for the future. They looked like chalk and cheese as they smiled and laughed with each other. It was evident, just in the way the two friends dressed and held themselves that Zoe was the more simplistic soul, dressing in simple t -shirts, shorts and flip flops with her hair cut in a neat dark bob. Tia, on the other hand, preened her hair each morning, arranging her permed curls with a noxious blast of hair spray. She still wore her kitten heels and padded shoulder box jackets, teamed with a below the knee pencil skirt.
'So, I think you three ladies need an early night. You must arrive at 6 am no later to the kafenion 'Alexis' on the road from Iraepetra to Ferma. . There you will wait until you are picked up and you must go with your manager for a day working in the thermokipion, I think

A Lock up on Crete

they call them green houses in English. Do not mention my name as it is illegal for foreigners to work in Greece, especially here in Crete.'

'Thank you Fotis. We won't let you down,' chimed Mel, Zoe and Tia as they took it in turns to shake his hand. They made the short way back to the apartment for a siesta as two males walked the same way keeping a permissible distance until they arrived at the foyer of their apartment.

'Andreas. Damianos. What are you two doing here?' asked Mel as she opened the door to the foyer, allowing Zoe and Tia to enter.

'Zoe, please wait one moment.' Damianos beckoned for her to come closer. Zoe turned on the stairway and opened the glass door slightly.

'I want to tell you that girl in the bar you saw me with the first night you arrived. She's nothing to me. She has returned to Sweden. I would like to meet you tomorrow.'

'We're starting work tomorrow.' Zoe looked to the ceiling at the ornate light fitting and continued. 'If I am not too tired, I will let you know.'

Zoe closed the door to a slightly disappointed Damianos as Andreas handed her a scribbled note.

'Please give this to Tia.'

With a glimmer of hope written across their faces, Andreas and Damianos turned on their heels and headed back into town.

Back in the apartment, a slight tension had risen between the three friends as Mel made an announcement.

A Lock up on Crete

'Tia, Zoe. I don't want to preach but please be careful with the locals. I know they seem friendly and they mostly are, but I have been here before and I have been hurt. After all we are new in town and with the summer tourists gone, we are a bit of a novelty. Please for all our sakes can we make a pact and agree that we don't allow any males to stay overnight in this apartment? It's the only way I can see it working out to be honest.'
'Absolutely Mel,' Zoe replied as Mel looked toward Tia, who was re- reading her note from Andreas.
'Yes, yes. Me too'

The alarm clock almost jumped from Mel's bedside table onto the floor as it shrilled and vibrated announcing the fifth hour of a new day in Iraepetra, the greenhouse capital of Crete. Despite the early hour, the three friends diligently took turns in the bathroom before locking their door for the day and walking down to kafenion Alexis, the meeting place for workers and employers alike. Although never advertised as such, the kafenion opened at 4am to service the many greenhouse owners looking for labourers, the majority who were illegal transient touristees.
Tia was taken first. She'd only just started to sip her Nescafe when a middle aged male with a snow white handle bar moustache whisked her away in his pickup truck. Rather irritated but spurred on by Mel, she dutifully followed and took her seat next to the driver - her employer for the day.
'This is like being picked for a school sports team,' Zoe commented as Mel was beckoned forward by a slim

A Lock up on Crete

male with blonde curly hair whom recognised her from four years ago. Zoe watched as Mel followed him to his truck. A few minutes later Mel still hadn't got into the truck as she continued to engage in animated conversation with a lot of hand gestures that pointed at Zoe. Finally, Mel shrugged her shoulders and mouthed 'sorry' through the window to her friend who was now feeling like that kid who was the last one left to be picked for the team. Finally, Zoe was approached by a short man with a mop of greying hair and asked to go outside where she was introduced to her new employer, a heavy set woman who didn't move from her driver's seat.

'This is Despoina. She does not speak any English so you will have to speak Greek. She will pay you at the end of the day and provide your meals. She will return you here. She is a good lady,' the short man explained as he clamped his hands around Zoe's backside and hauled her into the hard metal exterior of the pickup.

Later that day the three women arrived back at the apartment within minutes of each other. Cramped around the small kitchen table, Mel handed the bottle of Retsina wine to Zoe who promptly twisted the corkscrew and poured three small glasses. Tia's expression said it all as to warrant the need for alcohol at five in the afternoon.

'So, how was your day, Tia?' asked Mel breaking the silence that had descended in the small kitchen.

'I can't do it. I felt like a bloody animal carted off for slaughter in that truck. No, in fact I felt like a prostitute

A Lock up on Crete

the way we were selected at that filthy kafenion and herded away. No, sorry but it's not for me. I'll stay until my money runs out then I'll go back home!' Tia gulped down her second glass of Retsina. 'Sorry and all of that but I'm just not suited for this kind of work,'she added as she replaced the looped earrings in her ears.

'But what about Andreas?' Zoe piped up. Zoe knew how much he meant to her that night when she had witnessed them struck by the thunderbolt outside those rancid toilets.

'I'll ask him to come back home with me,' she breezed as Mel swept away the bottle of Retsina and returned it to the fridge. Mel felt slightly responsible for her two friends as it had been her suggestion to bring them here and was saddened that Tia seemed to be giving up after the first day of work. She also felt a pang of annoyance as she had worked hard to try get them all work and it seemed that Tia hadn't really given it a chance.

'My day was horrendous but I'll be going back again in the morning.' Zoe filled them in about her fateful first day tending the cucumber plants. A few moments later, Mel returned the wine to the table as the mood lifted and all three women screamed with laughter as Zoe recalled her experience.

'Oh my God and then, after about an hour of being all alone in that huge red hot greenhouse, wondering what on earth I was supposed to be pruning from the cucumber plants, I heard little murmurings and stifled giggles coming from somewhere nearby. At first I thought it may have been some kids having a laugh so I

A Lock up on Crete

parted the green leaves and saw a Honda 50 scooter parked up in the next row.'

'Ohh I bet you were creeped out, were you?' Tia asked, her mood lightening with every sip of wine.

'Yeah, a little. I thought someone was playing a prank on me to be honest as I didn't have a clue how I was supposed to be pruning the plants. The only tuition I'd had from the big Greek woman at the start of the day was her rambling on in Greek as she twisted a few leaves and pulled off curly bits that grew in between the stalk. She kept saying Ne ne and shaking her head. I assumed she was trying to say No, no, so I kept saying Yes, yes, nodding my head. Well it all got a bit confusing so she pulled at my arm and almost dragged me to a crumbling white hut in the middle of the greenhouse. It was weird because it was a proper stone hut plonked in the middle of the huge greenhouse.'

'That would have the main house originally and then the greenhouse would have been built around it,' Mel explained as Zoe and Tia raised their eyebrows in unison.

'Well anyway, she opened the door which was half hanging on its hinges. Then she grunted and showed me the fridge and gestured with her hands to her mouth that whatever was in it I could eat. I thought she meant it was my break as I sat down at the table until she wrote 1pm on a piece of paper. I nodded and followed her back to the row I had been working on wondering if I'd be able to find my way back through the maze of rows to the hut.' Zoe paused as she hauled another bottle of retsina from the fridge and poured a touch more into their glasses.

A Lock up on Crete

'Anyway, back to the shenanigans in the greenhouse. So, like an intrepid explorer I started to step from one row to another leaving a trail of flower heads that I'd picked out of a wheelbarrow behind me to find my way back. Then I saw them. Big, tall Greek woman and a very short police man getting amorous between the cucumber plants!'

'Oh this just gets better. Carry on,' Mel interrupted as she handed out some dry crackers and feta cheese.

'So, just as I was tiptoeing back through the rows, the giggling stopped and big tall Greek woman began shouting *Zoe, Zoe*. I guess it was easy for her to remember my name as it means 'Life' in Greek. Anyway, thankful to have found my way back to the row I had been working on, I answered with a curt 'Ne, ne' which after consulting with my phrase book, I realised it meant Yes not No. Oh, I forgot to mention my lunch. Let me tell you about that before I continue. When I'd found my way back to the stone hut, I opened the fridge door and found a tub of yogurt. I opened it up hoping to find some honey to pour into it only to find an army of ants marching all over it! I then resorted to reaching at the back for a tin of squid. Well you know me and seafood! I found a tin opener and reluctantly opened the tin and nearly wretched all over myself. The smell was putrid as I ran out of the hut back to the row of cucumbers. I desperately needed the loo and was just about to pull my shorts down as the Big Greek woman strode over the rows like a giant. All I could see as I crouched there were two gigantic feet. Fortunately I managed to stand up straight with my shorts where they should be as she

A Lock up on Crete

started yelling at me pointing to the plants and wagging her finger. All I could decipher was that I had been pruning the wrong bits as she held up the curly bits and threw them at me. I heard the scooter start up and then she marched me out to her truck, handed me some cash and delivered me back to Alexis' kafenion without asking if I was available tomorrow!'

'Mmm maybe my day wasn't so bad after all,' Tia chuckled as a loud knock on the door broke their conversation.

Andreas stood at the door looking pristine in his light coloured trousers teamed with a navy blue short sleeved shirt and a smattering of gel to his unruly blond curls. 'Ready, Tia?' he asked, as Tia bustled to the door and ordered him to wait in the foyer for five minutes.

'Hell, I didn't think he'd actually be on time!' Tia shrilled, swapping her work clothes for a cream coloured twin set, accessorised by a chunky black necklace and an application of red lipstick. Zoe and Mel exchanged smiles watching Tia fuss about her outfit, knowing full well she looked stunning.

'I don't want to sound negative, but if Tia can't hack it here can you really imagine Andreas leaving all this great weather and gorgeous island behind? Tia told me that where she lived it was in a valley and it was known as the rainiest place in Scotland!' Mel nodded and added her spin on it:

'From past experience you can take the Cretan away from Crete but you can't take the Crete out of a Cretan.' Both girls sat in silence for a while before a loud knock on the door snapped them out of their reverie. Zoe gingerly made her way to the door, hoping it was not Damianos. She had told Tia to tell Andreas to tell Damianos, that if they saw him that she would not be meeting him that night. Instinctively, Zoe turned all the lights off and grabbed her thin dressing gown and pulled it around her clothes. She opened the door to where Damianos was standing, looking very attractive as the moon cast a glow over him from the window in the hallway.

'Damianos, we are in bed now. I need lots of sleep when I'm working so maybe I will come out at the weekend,' Zoe explained as she put her hand to her mouth as if to stifle a yawn.

'You English go to bed early!' Damianos shrugged his shoulders and promptly took the stairs out of the apartment.

'Well that went well!' Zoe relayed to Mel as they ventured onto the balcony with a glass of water. It was eerily quiet as they spotted Damianos as he sauntered down the deserted street with his hands stuffed in his pockets. He gave a backward glance to the apartment then took the corner to the seafront.

'Sometimes I wish we had a television but then I suppose it would all be in Greek anyway.' Zoe thought out loud as she returned to her bed and opened her book. Mel sat on the balcony for a while, lost in thought as a few teenagers broke the silence and screeched up and down the road on their mopeds.

<u>6 am at Alexis Kafenion, Iraepetra</u>

A Lock up on Crete

'These women are thieves. Do not give jobs.' Apollonia's announcement, first in Greek for the benefit of the elderly locals who furiously clacked their kolomboli - worry beads, then repeated in English. Her vitriol resonated through the kafenion.

Mel rose from the plastic chair towering above Apollonia.

'Signoma se parakalo. Poios eisai? – Excuse me, who are you?' Mel questioned, pleased she still remembered some Greek phrases.

'I am Apollonia from Agios Nikolaos and I am here to take back to my good friend Manolis Mariakis a 10,000 drachma note from you that is not fake like the one you gave him.'

Alexis, the owner of the kafenion turned the music down as the kafenion fell deathly silent. The older men leant a little more forward, willing their old ears to hear more clearly.

'I am sorry but I do not know who this Manolis is nor do I know of any fake drachma note. You have clearly mistaken us for other people,' Mel replied slowly in case the old lady didn't understand her accent.

'You paid for your meal in friend's kafenion last week with this fake note and I know it is you three as I remember seeing you arrive in Agios Nikolaos and also know where you stayed,' Apollonia's English was perfect. The older woman threw her shoulders back and raised her head as if to square up to Mel, her younger adversary.

'Yes, we were there but we did not give a fake note to this Manolis. Also, how did you know we were here in

Iraepetra?' Tia demanded as she stood up next to Mel while Zoe followed suit.

'Ha, nothing gets past a Cretan.' Apollonia gestured with a wave of her hand as if she was pointing to some God or Goddess up above. She didn't answer Tia's question. She wasn't about to tell them how she had followed them as soon as they arrived and had her ear to the door of the room they had stayed in. Silence hung in the air as she commended herself on her exceptional memory. Apollonia, at one time, thought she was becoming senile but she was of the opinion that the longer one worked the longer you kept your wits about you. However, she had noticed Manolis had become forgetful of late and actually wondered whether or not he had mixed up the fake note. But she liked a challenge; it kept her young and so she continued her accusations. 'Pah, you think you come here and nobody notices you?' She directed her eagle like eyes on Zoe who, as yet she hadn't joined in with the verbal altercation. Keep them thinking that Cretan eyes were watching their every move from now on, Apollonia told herself as she took a step back from the taller girl. 'Be aware, we watch you touristees that come to our island in the winter. Give me the 10,000 drachma and I will take it to my friend Manolis and I will tell him not to take the fake one to the police.'

A few older men exchanged confused faces as Alexis deliberated whether to ask Apollonia to leave his premises or the three touristees. Before he made his decision he asked his locals if they knew of this woman, Apollonia. Two men raised their eyes to the smoke smeared ceiling and another one circled his finger to his temple. He waited for a few minutes before retreating into the back of the counter and punching some numbers in his telephone.

Nobody was standing down from the altercation as Zoe and Tia stood either side of Mel realising the old lady, all 5 foot of her was not for leaving without an admission of guilt and a replacement drachma note, which Tia had calculated to be worth around £30. Zoe cast a sideways glance towards the blue wooden door and recognised the tubby policeman from the greenhouse the other day, accompanied by a younger and handsome colleague. At first they struggled to comprehend the situation at hand until the older one recognised Apollonia from the mug shot book, spanning two decades, back at the police station. He rubbed his chin amazed that she was still at it! The touristee girls must have been on her patch, Yiorgos mused as he glanced again at the touristee with the black bob, wondering where he had seen her before.

The three girls looked on in disbelief when Apollonia relayed her accusation to the policemen. One by one, the girls were escorted out to the police van and swiftly taken to the police station for further questioning.

'I honestly did not hand over a fake 10,000 drachma note. I remember the bill only came to 2,000 drachmas and I gave him a 2,000 drachma note and even threw a few coins in his bloody tip jar,' Mel insisted as the taller policeman took her fingerprints.

'Excuse us but why are you not taking our fingerprints?' Zoe and Tia moved in closer to Mel forming a human

A Lock up on Crete

safety net as they reinforced Mel's account of the preposterous accusation Apollonia had made.

'Ladies. I am the tourist policeman here in Ierapetra. Please, if you just conform, we will get these prints off to Agios Nikolaos police station tomorrow and we will compare them with the prints on the fake note. That is of course that the note is at the police station. I can assure you all that this will be sorted soon. But I do have to ask you not to go back to the worker kafenion. It is illegal for tourists to work here in Crete. I will personally come to tell you the results of the fingerprints when I know. And remember I am here to help you. You are staying at Theo's, is that right?' The three girls nodded as they followed each other out of the bright blue double doors of the police station, incongruously positioned in the middle of the shopping area.

'Bloody hell, we've not really made a good start here have we? I mean, what are we going to do for work now? Everyone will know now who we are and that we are potential criminals.'

'Calm down Zoe. Did you not see the tourist policeman give us a wink when he told us it was illegal to work? They all know they need touristees to work in the greenhouses so if we just take a couple of days off and go back to Alexis in a few days it will all be yesterday's news and I'm certain that my fingerprints will not be on the fake note. Why do you think he only took my prints?' Mel assured her friends as they made their way back to the apartment and Zoe revealed her own thoughts to her two friends.

A Lock up on Crete

'I like the men folk here but I'm not too sure about the women folk. First there was big woman from the greenhouse yesterday and now this little witch from the launderette trying to get us into trouble. And can you believe she came all the way from Agios Nikolaos and hunted us down to make a scene like she did? Why didn't she just leave it up to the police?' Out of habit more than hunger, they stopped off at the corner shop close to the apartment for a cheese and spinach pie. They waited for the spanakopita to cool down as they sat on the traditional wooden chairs catching a few weak rays of winter sun while Mel explained.

'The Cretans are extremely protective of each other, especially the older ones. They have been through a lot of hardship in their lives with the German invasion of WW2 to the civil war. It's intrinsic to them to fight for what they believe in and if Apollonia really did follow us when we arrived in Agios Nikolaos she would have assumed that we would be looking for work at Alexis's. Mind you, she must have woken earlier than us unless she doesn't sleep well and she must have already been in town as she couldn't possibly have arrived all the way from Agios Nikolaos that early.' Mel hoped she was assuring her friends as they tucked into the pies then attempted to make light of the situation recalling how she had used her little bit of Greek to confront Apollonia at Alexis's. The three girls laughed as they took stock of how they had already made a significant mark on the town of Iraepetra.

'You couldn't write it!' Tia chuckled as she stopped at the kiosk and bought three bars of chocolate. 'That job search was even shorter lived than the job centre back home,' Zoe piped up as she accepted her chocolate bar from Tia.

Mel popped a piece into her mouth knowing full well that it was far too early to be savouring the delights of the Greek milk chocolate; she also knew it would release some much needed serotonin. After the third piece, although they had not made the best start workwise, she felt her worries melt away and reassured herself that she had done the right thing in suggesting they travel to find work in Iraepetra. Besides, she had a personal reason to be here once again: she had heard that a certain male, according to Damianos was due to return soon from Cyprus.

10 am that same day

Along with most of the inhabitants of Ireapetra, word had reached Andreas and Damianos who turned up together at the girls' apartment door. In accordance with the girls' agreement, the boys remained at the doorway as the girls stood opposite.

'Koritsis, Girls. We hear about what happened at Alexis' Are you all ok?' a worried Andreas asked.

'Yes we are well, just a little mix up,' replied Zoe as she scanned Damianos up and down in his rather pristine work clothes.

'This woman. I think I know of her. A bit of a body busy. You will not be taking any more shit from her,' Andreas added, placing his hand on Tia's shoulder as she inched forward to the door. 'Leave your work for a few days girls and I will make some asking if there is any work

A Lock up on Crete

around. I am the supervisor of the flower factory,'
Damianos affirmed as he and Andreas left to return to
their work. Zoe was still reeling from the image of
Damianos in his work gear and hoped they could get
work in the flower factory- at least it would smell nice.
'Andreas, do you think we will ever be invited into their
room?' Damianos asked as they walked down the stairs.
Andreas shrugged his shoulders as if it was a forgone
conclusion.

Chapter 4

A few days later
Old Manolis Mariakis
The tourist policeman returned as promised with the
results of the fingerprints. Old Manolis had been
questioned as to why he hadn't taken the note to the
bank to check its authenticity. Apparently, he had
misplaced the note after showing it to Apollonia who
just happened to be passing his kafenion on her way
from the bus station. He added that he needed to talk to
her as he owed her money and so showed her the note
which he thought she had taken. He did admit that he
had been foolish in stirring up all the bother and didn't
think she would take it that far. He recalled to the
policeman how he had been enamoured with her for
years but knew it would never work out due to the way
she received her income. He reflected how she had been
an absolute stunner as a young woman but had never
married and had rebuked his proposal; he had thus

A Lock up on Crete

resigned himself to the fact that he would never be able to tell Apollonia how he felt about her, despite her work. Maybe he was getting too old for all this? Maybe he should get in touch with his nephew Andreas in Iraepetra and hand over the business sooner rather than later. He could retire fully to his little white washed cottage and the view of the turquoise sea that he could watch change with the seasons and weather. If truth be told, he feared for his mental wellbeing and memory. All he had ever wanted was to be with Apollonia, despite her chequered past.

Mel knew from previous experience that there would be a minority of the inhabitants of Iraepetra who would believe the three touristees were up to no good and they would need to prove their innocence with the older generation if they were to stay and be respected. Tia and Zoe had become a little downhearted after their exit had been noticed from the police station so she decided to treat them to a meal at the taverna near the port which specialised in fresh fish. The afternoon chatter became slightly louder with each bottle of Retsina as a middle aged male after approached their table smiling from ear to ear.

'Hey Meli Meli, is it really you? Your curls are longer and oh your hair is lighter in colour but I know it is you. Are you here to work again in my kitchen?'

'Phew, Mr M, slow down, slow down. Let me introduce you to my two friends, Tia and Zoe.'

Mel's ex- boss who she always referred to as Mr M, short for Medusa, pumped their hands respectively as he turned his attention once more to Mel as she offered him a seat.

'And yes we are all looking for work but if I work in your kitchen again I want to do more than wash dishes. How about me baking some pastries for your customers? But you have to find work for my friends too,' Mel demanded of her potential employer. He nodded in agreement and wrote down a name and number for a work contact and handed it to Zoe.

'Meli! You start tomorrow. I will tell my wife to find the baking things.'

Mid November Iraepetra

Fortunately, true to his word, Mr M   welcomed Mel back to his restaurant 'Medusa' where she learnt the highly respected skill of making Filo pastry. It felt good to be back in the kitchen with her pastry ingredients and to feel the soft touch of flour as she handled the delicate pastry, every now and again throwing in a bit of an English twist to it. Soon the locals were drooling over her fresh Bakewell tarts and Apple pies smothered in custard. Mr M was impressed with the orders for her baking he was receiving and asked if she would like more hours. It seemed that the majority of orders for her baking were coming from as far as Heraklion in the north. Whatever or whoever had been responsible for the sudden increase in demand for the young English touristee's baking, Mr M was equally bemused and grateful. Mel accepted the increased hours but insisted that she have a full hour for her lunch and weekends off.

A Lock up on Crete

At lunch she would take her daily walk along the lively café and bar lined seafront until she reached the small port. There she would watch the fishermen wrestling with their nets as the November winds whipped up the waves crashing into the sea wall. Mel loved the smell of Iraepetra; the distinct smell and taste of the salty sea, the fresh air and the whole busy vibe of the working town. A few days later, Zoe and Tia started working in the cucumber factory on the outskirts of town with a few more tourists and a gaggle of older local women. They were picked up promptly at six am and herded into a pickup truck with a cover over, cramming in what seemed like the whole of the work force of Iraepetra.

The cucumber factory
'Oh bloody hell, trust us to have to work alongside these lot,' Tia muttered to Zoe as they took their place at the huge crate, filled to the brim with dusty cucumbers. She referred to the group of older local women clad in their drab housecoats and hairnets. Their beady eyes followed them around like hawks. Zoe wished that Damianos had been able to find them work in the flower factory instead but she hadn't heard from him for a while. After a cold reception from their colleagues, Tia turned to Zoe as they stood side by side.
'Surely they haven't heard about the fake 10,000 drachma note debacle, do you think Zoe?'
'Probably,' Zoe sighed as she accepted the square piece of yellow foam from one of the women with a pleasant thank you 'Efcharisto.'

By lunchtime, both girls were proficient in the art of cleaning cucumbers. They had even managed to make a few of the women smile when Tia selected a rotten cucumber from the vat and threw it in the air in disgust as it fell apart in a heap of mush. Soon after, Zoe had had a cucumber mishap as she leant in the near empty vat and lost her balance nearly ending up with the remaining cucumbers. Even the sternest looking woman had cracked a smirk!

They lunched in the olive groves opposite the factory with the Cretan women. They seemed to have warmed to the new 'touristees' as the day progressed as they fed them like they were their own children with cold meatballs, bright white feta cheese and plump, red beef tomatoes.

'Maybe we have won them over with our cucumber mishaps,' Zoe mused as she declined her second baklava from the octogenarian with the flowery head scarf and snow white hair.

 'I think we have cracked them Zoe. We should be ok working here,' Tia replied as she gingerly accepted a sticky pastry from the matriarch of the Greek women whose stained housecoat was in need of a 90 degree wash!

'Yeah I agree. The bosses seem decent enough blokes too. Have you seen those two tourist lads though? They work at the far end of the packing machine? They seem a bit shifty to me so I think we should stick with these old dears, don't you Tia?'

'Absolutley,' Tia agreed, as she washed down her lunch with a huge slice of water melon.

A Lock up on Crete

As the days became shorter and the sun weaker, the three girls worked hard and won back their respect from the townsfolk of Iraepetra. Winter in Crete was good. They had a nice apartment, good jobs and plenty of friends around town. And the most important thing was they were there for one another and similarly had one another's upmost respect.

December - A new addition
Since leaving the idyllic island of Guernsey, the girls had kept in touch with another friend Cara, who was eager to join them for the winter. Each day the girls would take it in turns to go to the post office to check if there was any mail for them. Amongst the regular letters from their families and friends, Mel was pleased to receive news of Cara's imminent arrival.
'I suppose we should ask Theo for a four bedroom room for when Cara arrives,' Tia suggested as they sat having their weekly treat of Mel's pudding at Medusa's. Mel was surprised to see so many of her raspberry pies still in packaging on the shelf in the kitchen as she passed to go to the toilet. She thought the majority had all been sold that day and had purposely put one away for them under the counter. If they weren't sold soon they wouldn't keep their freshness overnight. She was perplexed and reminded herself to ask Mr M the next morning.
Zoe broke into her thoughts as she focussed again on her friends as she returned from the toilet.

A Lock up on Crete

'I just hope it doesn't upset the balance,' Zoe shifted in her chair as the young waitress set the pies and cream on the table. 'I mean it will be great to have Cara here but we three get on so well I wouldn't want it to upset anything.'

'Well I think we will just have to set down our house rules from the outset. I did share a room with Cara in Guernsey and thankfully she doesn't snore or sleepwalk so we should all get on,' Mel added as Zoe wished she hadn't broached the subject. Tia seemed preoccupied as she fiddled with her beads on her necklace. She still kept up her impeccable appearance - much to the bewilderment of Zoe and Mel. In fact, as soon as she arrived home from work each day, even when she was only chatting with Andreas in the hallway, she would carefully select her lounging outfit while Zoe and Mel reached for their trusted joggers. Tia prided herself on her select collection of accessories and knew that Andreas was proud to take her out, even if it was only to his friend's taverna a few miles up the coast road.

Cara Matthews, Bristol, England

Cara eventually secured a loan that would set her free on the road to Crete. She knew she shouldn't have done it. It was wrong but she was so lonely and couldn't bear the thought of another winter on her own in the damp caravan of her late parents. The only relatives lived an hour away and she had never bothered with her cousins. Her only brother lived in America but moved so often with his job it was hard to keep in touch with him. At the tender age of twenty, loneliness ripped through her heart every morning but she knew she hid it well. On reflection, the summer had been the tonic she so desperately needed where she had met Tia, Mel and Zoe at the Seaview hotel. One night, she had heard them at the bar where she was working her shift, planning a trip to Crete for the winter. Back on the caravan retirement site, sat around the small electric heater, she leafed through her address book and spotted Zoe's UK address. A week later, she had a reply from Zoe's mother giving her the address of the Poste restante in Iraepetra.

Cara travelled first from the caravan in Devon to Bristol where her cousin lived and applied through a loan shark advertised in the Bristol Evening Echo. She searched for hours in the back streets of the city, periodically looking over her shoulder. Within minutes, Cara was walking back out of the dingy office with cash pound notes. She felt almost rich; her parents left nothing in their will and the caravan was worthless. Cara knew that she would probably have to pay for it to be scrapped one day but for now it was a base. She also knew she had to be frugal with the money and set off to Crete as soon as she could. Unbeknown to Cara, the girls had been religiously waiting each morning in turn at the bus station to await her arrival. After the fourth day and with no letter at the post restante, they stopped going. After all, if Cara did arrive and they weren't there, there would undoubtedly be a multitude of people who would know who she was already; word would quickly be passed on to Mel at the restaurant or if it was evening, someone would give Cara directions to the girls apartment block.

A Lock up on Crete

It was on a cool but dry Tuesday evening when Cara eventually arrived in Iraepetra. Not knowing where she was heading, she was more than relieved when the bus driver asked if she was the English girls' friend. Her reply being yes she was but one of the girls was Scottish. With a slight furrow of his brow he told Cara to stay on the bus. When the last passenger had climbed down from the steep steps, he drove her round the corner to the apartment. Mel was on the balcony taking in her underwear from the make shift line when the bus screeched to a stop.

'Mel, Mel, it's me! Cara. I'm here!'

'About bloody time! Come on up – third floor, first door on the right. I'll put the kettle on,' Mel shrilled.

'So what took you so long Cara,' a sleepy Tia asked as they huddled round the compact but slighter bigger kitchen than the previous room.

'Oh, Jesus! Would you believe it? Well to cut a long story short I was on the coach and we had just been for a toilet break in a village somewhere near Milan,' Cara started.

'Excuse me but did you say you travelled by coach,' asked an incredulous Tia.

'Yes, yes, it was a bargain. Only cost 40 pounds all the way from London to Athens then I got the boat from Piraeus to Heraklion then the coach to here.' Cara asked for another cup of tea as Zoe rinsed the cups again.

'Anyway, as I was saying, we all got back on the coach and about two hours into our journey I had a horrible feeling that something was missing. I searched through my backpack so many times but I just couldn't find it. I

A Lock up on Crete

searched on my body and in my pockets but still I couldn't find it. Eventually I plucked up the courage to ask the driver to drive back,' Cara recalled as she stifled a yawn.

'Sorry but I'm not with you. What exactly were you looking for?' Zoe asked.

'Ahh Jesus, sorry girls. It was my passport. I thought I had lost it,' Cara hugged her cup of tea to her chest as the other girls took time to fathom out the dilemma.

'And did the coach driver go back,' Mel asked as she dunked a Greek shortbread she had just baked that day into her mug of tea.

'Ahh, can you believe it, he so did. We backtracked two hours back to the public toilets where I swore it may have fallen out of the top pocket of my backpack while I looked for a tissue. But as you can guess it wasn't there. Much to the annoyance of most of the bus passengers, we continued our journey. The coach driver advised that if it was still not found I should leave the bus at the next major city and go to the British consulate as there would be no chance I would be allowed into the neighbouring country of Yugoslavia without a passport. Oh girls it was horrible. I felt so helpless and alone.'

'So how long did it take to get a new passport then?' Mel asked as she shook her head.

'Oh, did I not say? All was well and I found my passport before we got to Verona in Italy.'

The three girls shook their head into their hands as Cara continued.

'So then I found the little begger of a passport under the seat of the coach. Well actually it was this cockney lad

A Lock up on Crete

who found it for me. I then had to creep up to the driver and tell him mid driving that all was well and my passport had been found.'

'Wow, you must be exhausted Cara,' reasoned Mel as she handed out another batch of shortbread.

'I can't believe the driver actually drove back to the toilets to be honest,' piped up Tia.

'Oh well, you're here now safe and sound and that's your bed over there. There's a spare towel in the bathroom,' added Zoe, as she rubbed the soles of her feet on the bedside mat she used before getting in bed.

The next morning Cara woke early as she struggled to get her bearings. She had struggled to sleep. She was still in travelling mode where she had been lulled to sleep by the controlled rhythm of the coach which she had been on since London. It had been awful saying goodbye when they finally arrived in Athens. As soon as he had taken over the wheel from Bob, a stout Yorkshire man, who had expertly driven them from London to Milan, there had been an instant attraction as she sat high up on the front seat looking down on the handsome new driver. Cara wondered if he would have turned back to Milan to find her passport if there hadn't been that attraction. She pulled her weary body from the bed and made herself a coffee in the kitchen before discovering the balcony at the back of the apartment. Her attention was diverted to the small garden below where a pair of brightly coloured birds flew between the shrubs. Cara Matthews hugged her coffee and thought back to the man she was missing already.

A Lock up on Crete

'I will write to you then at the post restante. Check the post office after one week and we will meet again one day soon,' he had urged as he gave her a lingering kiss at the coach station in Athens. She was woken from her reverie as Mel spotted her on the balcony asking if she needed a top up.

'How did you sleep Cara?' Mel dragged a kitchen chair onto the balcony.

'Ahh not too bad thanks. I'm not used to the comfort of a bed. I've been sitting up sleeping for the week but I was lucky and had the front seat of the coach to myself so I managed to curl up a little,' Cara explained as she stretched her arms and nearly sent the steaming mug of coffee flying. 'Oh Jesus I'm so clumsy, sorry Mel.'

'Get back in bed if you want. Zoe and Tia don't usually stir before eleven on a Sunday anyway. Hey, did you say you want to work while you are here Cara? The olive season is ready now and I have a few contacts if you like.'

Cara nodded as she made her way back to the bedroom she shared with Tia. She hadn't really got to know Tia much when they were in Guernsey so maybe Zoe and Mel had purposely put them together. She was just grateful that she was here and if she could find work even better; she had a good feeling about this town. In a few days she would remind herself to go to the poste restante. She might even stop pining over the coach driver whom she only knew of as Mr Milan; he had been quite elusive about his identity.

A Lock up on Crete

That evening, the girls, now four of them with the arrival of Cara, had an invitation from Mel's boss for all of them to attend his granddaughter's christening which was being held a short taxi ride at the side of the main road. All four friends wondered why the celebration was not held at the many seafront restaurants in Iraepetra. This was to be Cara's first night out with her friends and she felt glad that she had made the eventful journey as she tucked into a hearty salad followed by a meze of stuffed vine leaves and a dish that looked a bit like baby octopus or maybe a small part of a large octopus. Cara prided herself as having an international pallet and had even eaten sheep brains in Athens. It had been an impromptu meal to say thank you to the coach drivers. Although Cara's funds were low, she joined the other passengers at the roadside taverna. She personally felt the need to thank Mr Milan for his detour to find her passport. Within an hour the food was flowing quite literally onto the pavement. Cara being naturally clumsy had sat on her seat and nearly toppled over into the busy road. Instinctively she had grabbed hold of Mr Milan's shirt sleeve, bringing him down with her as they lay amongst the sheep brains in the gutter! If only she hadn't inherited her mother's clumsy trait; she could even hear her mother in her ear chiding her to be more careful.

The christening venue was fit to burst as young and old alike mingled with each other in animated conversation. Zoe, who had slight hearing loss didn't have to strain her ears at all in Greece. The Greeks did not have a volume

A Lock up on Crete

control and that suited Zoe fine as she was also a terrible lip reader.

After the last dishes were swept away, the four girls, under the slight influence of alcohol, enjoyed watching all the cute little Greek children receive their gifts from their parents and grandparents. As they all turned their attention to the children on the make shift dance floor decorated by strings of lights, a familiar, slightly stooped figure hobbled across to a vacant seat.

'Oh Lord. We can't seem to get away from that witch! Look, she's here again,' Tia exclaimed in a not so quiet voice.

'Oh yes it's her. She's the one that accused Mel, isn't she?' Zoe exclaimed as Damianos suddenly appeared holding the christening baby.

'Who we talking about, girls?' he asked as he looked around and waved at the witch.

'Do you know that old woman who has forgotten to take her hair net off?' Tia asked Damianos as he proceeded to hand her the baby while he stepped over the table to move closer to Zoe.

'Yes, of course I know most people here and that old woman is actually my aunt Apollonia and she is only 60,' he retorted as he waved again to his aunt who was pre occupied with devouring the free food like she hadn't eaten for a week.

'So why did you not say it was your aunt when she accused us of giving her friend Manolis a dodgy note,' Zoe asked as he sloped his arm around her back and searched for words.

'Oh to be truthful I thought you were talking about someone else when it happened. There is another woman in Iraepetra, very similar to my aunt.'
'Oh right,' Zoe replied as she moved a few inches from his hold and Tia swiftly changed the conversation.
'So why is Andreas not here then?' Tia asked.
'He said his family come first,' Damianos shrugged his shoulders as he excused himself to reach his aunt.
'That's a bit strange isn't it?' Zoe remarked as Tia nodded in agreement. Tia recalled Andreas saying he had some family business to take care of that night when she had spoken to him outside in the hall earlier on in the day.
'It's probably a long family feud that no one really knows why and when it started. You know a bit like Romeo and Juliet,' Mel explained as Tia rolled her eyes at the thought of being embroiled in a Greek Capulet and Montague feud. She reminded herself to broach the subject with Andreas sometime. After all, Andreas and Damianos had become quite pally just lately, turning up together at the girls apartment. Something didn't add up she thought as she helped herself to another glass of complimentary wine. The evening continued to show no signs of diminishing as the young children began to tire and sprawled themselves out on their parent's laps. The four girls, tired of stifling their yawns, agreed to leave, waving a goodbye to their busy host.
Damianos and his aunt were nowhere to be seen much to the relief of Zoe. She had decided that she didn't want to continue to see him. And if he asked, when she broached the subject, she would be honest and tell him

A Lock up on Crete

she was uneasy with him being related to Apollonia. She had also noticed from the christening that Apollonia had kept a low profile and had only conversed with her nephew, Damianos.

Cara and the man from Milan

The three girls had the pleasure of the company of the scatty, clumsy but amicable Cara for all of two weeks before she bid them farewell in her quest to find Mr Milan, the coach driver. True to his word, he had wrote to her at the post restante and asked if she would care to accompany him in Athens on his next trip and work with him on his coach journeys as a kind of hostess. She had had a few days working in the greenhouses as there were no vacancies at the cucumber factory and had unfortunately had the same experience as Zoe had with the big Greek lady. Thus, she was easily swayed into the offer from the man from Milan and excited to be reunited with him.

Zoe

Like Cara, Zoe was also embarking on an adventure. The day after they had said they goodbyes to Cara at the bus station, where they reminded her not to misplace her passport again, Zoe had a proposal from Damianos. He told her he would pay for her travel to Istanbul if she would accompany him and his friend Michalis.
'Why Istanbul? And why do you need me to go with you if your friend is going. And there's something else I have to tell you...'

A Lock up on Crete

'They have good leather clothes there and they are a good price. ' Damianos had clearly evaded Zoe's questions as he took her hand in his to cross the road. 'We travel with the best tour company and stay in some nice hotels with food. It will be an experience,' he continued as they walked the short distance from the main road to Fotis's café bar.

Zoe settled into the comfy outdoor chairs as she zipped up her jacket and forgot about her intentions to call it off with Damianos. Istanbul sounded quite exciting all of a sudden.

'How long will we be gone for as I will have to see if I can get the time off from the factory,' Zoe asked as he took a strand of hair that had settled over her eye and carefully curled it around her ear.

'Well I have a surprise for you,' he continued, ordering Zoe a Metaxa brandy to warm her up. 'I was offered a job at the cucumber factory today. I said I could start when we return from Istanbul. So you do not need to ask your bosses. It is all arranged.' Zoe couldn't speak. She didn't know how to react. Should she throw her arms around him or exercise caution? Her stomach settled the dilemma as she excused herself to go to the loo.

In the loo she splashed some cold water on her face. The mirror was one of those cheap ones as she looked at her distorted reflection. *Is this relationship with Damianos dangerous? Is it really what you want Zoe? Is he a little too intense for you? Remember you are only 20 – a free spirit and all that.*

Usually a conversation with herself in the mirror gave her clarity but the distortion of her features were

A Lock up on Crete

freaking her out as she dried her face on a stray tissue she found in her jeans pocket.

Chapter 5

On the road to Istanbul, middle of December, 1984

Fortunately for Zoe, Cara had left some winter clothes behind when she set off on her adventure with the man from Milan. Zoe chose a light pink sweat shirt. As she pulled it over her head, something fell out of the front pocket. She picked it up and turned it over. It was a one year British passport which looked like it had definitely been through the washing machine with water stained crinkled pages. The image of Cara smiling into the camera was also distorted by the water damage but it was unmistakably her face. If Cara was still in Greece, she wouldn't have realised that she had left her passport behind – Again! If they had already reached the Greek/Albanian border on route to Italy then she would be frantically searching her bags again for her passport. Oh Cara, what are you like? But how on earth was she to get it to her now? She let out a sigh as she realised that Tia and Zoe could deal with it while she went to Istanbul. She would leave a note for them – there might already be a letter at the post restante from Cara. She smiled as she wondered what the lovable but scatty Cara

A Lock up on Crete

was up to now. Looking over the passport one more time before she placed it in her bedroom drawer, she noticed Cara's name: Zoe Matthews.

'What the hell! What's going on here?' Zoe said out loud. 'Why is she using my name on her passport? She's Cara Matthews; I'm Zoe Matthews! Why has she called herself Cara instead of her real name? Why has she never mentioned she has the exact same name as me? I am Zoe Matthews,' she reminded herself just in case she was losing it. 'Who the hell is she?' Zoe added the discovery to the note alerting the girls of Cara's true identity. Maybe they could ask the tourist policeman his opinion? A shiver sprinted up and down her back as she looked at the time. 'Hell, I'd better get a move on. Damianos is picking me up in ten minutes.' She left the passport on top of her drawer and checked hers and then checked again that it definitely was hers with her name on it: Zoe Matthews. She then took Cara's sweat shirt out of her bag and threw it in the wardrobe – she didn't want to wear it anymore that was for sure. Damianos would be picking her up any minute now as he had arranged a lift to Heraklion where they would board the ferry to Athens. From Athens they would join a coach party which would take them all the way to Istanbul, passing Thessaoniki, Greece's second largest city. A horn honked below as she closed the door behind her and took a deep breath. She wanted to stay and work out the riddle of Cara with Mel and Tia. But she couldn't let Damianos down at this late stage. She would try not to think too deeply into it and enjoy her trip to

A Lock up on Crete

Istanbul. As she stuffed the last of her cosmetics into her bag she wondered if it was a mere coincidence or something more incriminating.

Greek/Turkish border Pasakoy

'Do you think I look like a criminal,' a Greek coach passenger asked Zoe at 2am in the morning as they waited in line at the border control.

'Ermm no not at all but maybe it's your heavy beard. Maybe if you had shaved.' Zoe shrugged her shoulders and turned round before he responded to see that Damianos and Michalis had been singled out from the line by a guard with an elaborate moustache which was far too heavy for his narrow head.

'Now why do they take the two boys away? Do you think they look like criminals?

'No they don't either but it is probably because you are from Greece,' Zoe shrugged again surprised at her reply as she held her passport tight to her chest feeling a little immune with her British passport. She willed herself not to think about Cara's passport but couldn't help wondering if she had somehow stolen her identity.

'We hate each other,' the lady with the man explained as a female guard passed by with a machine gun strapped over her shoulder. Zoe couldn't believe the stupidity of the Greek man unless he thought that by speaking English they wouldn't understand him; maybe the Turks didn't speak English very well? Who knows? All Zoe was bothered about was the return of Damianos and Michalis from their interrogation and her own

A Lock up on Crete

safeguarding. The Greek man, if he continued to be so stupid, would just have to suffer the consequences. Damianos and Michalis returned to the line just as Zoe was showing her passport to the Customs man in the heavily armoured kiosk - he waved her through without any scrutiny of her identity.

'So I take it you two nations do not really get on?' Zoe remarked as Damianos and Michalis joined her at the other side of the border control.

'Yes, we hate each other but don't take it the wrong way. We will be safe,' Zoe wasn't completely reassured as she secured her revered passport in her cross over travel bag. *We will be safe.* Damianos' phrase echoed in her ears as she tried to remain optimistic. Zoe didn't have much knowledge about the deep rooted fractured relationship between the Greeks and the Turks but it was very unpleasant to be in the midst of it. Again, she should have trusted her instincts and stayed in Iraepetra. She looked around the coach at the sleeping Greek faces, wondering who they were and why would they decide to go on an organised coach holiday to a neighbouring country you were at loggerheads with. It was too late to turn back now though!

Michalis proved to be a welcome travelling companion, chatting easily among his fellow Greeks and interpreting for Zoe. He spoke of his difficulty at school with having dyslexia which he informed her was a Greek word meaning *non-reading*. Nevertheless, he had learned different skills and eventually took over his Uncle's souvlaki stand and to date was very successful at both the business and his culinary skills. In fact his homemade tzatziki was reputed to be the best in the south of Crete.

'Michalis, why have you come on this trip when you know how hostile you two nations are with each other,' Zoe asked as they were herded off the bus to a designated outdoor area.

'Like Damianos, I buy leather which is much better and cheaper than in Greece. Iraepetra is cold in the winter. He asked me to go with him before he met you.'

'Oh crap! I feel like a gooseberry now,' Zoe said as she looked around for Damianos, who seemed very edgy.

'Zoe what is this gooseberry. Whatever it is I don't think you look like one. Is it like a blackberry?' Michalis replied as Damianos reappeared in the line. Zoe broke into a huge smile and translated the idiom to Michalis, who she was growing quite fond of.

After following instructions to take off their shoes and place them in a plastic tray to be checked by the coach driver, they were herded back on the coach. Zoe didn't have a clue nor the energy to ask why the seemingly futile operation had just taken place.

The Grand Bazaar, Istanbul

The Grand Bazaar was indeed grandiose, adorned with bespoke stalls under an ornate deep yellow domed roof selling a plethora of items from leather purses to intricate rugs. Heady spices filled the air. Young boys meandered through the crowds with trays of mint tea delivering to the potential customers whom had been enticed into the shops.

A Lock up on Crete

'It's crazy isn't it Zoe?' Damianos said with a new light in his eyes as he gripped her hand making their way to the leather area. Michalis had stopped at a jewellery shop to try on an oversize watch.

'Just a bit,' she replied already tiring of it. In fact she wished she was back in her apartment in Crete. She was tired of feeling uncomfortable and constantly watching her back. She might have been experiencing a different reception if she wasn't with the Greek party but still she was jaded.

To top it off, Damianos was much worse than a woman shopping. She felt like the roles had been reversed as she sat on the colourful chaise longue as Damianos changed numerous times relentlessly asking her opinion. She was actually waiting for him to say, *Does my bum look big in these*?

That evening they dined in the hotel with the coach party and once again Michalis interpreted for her as he informed her that he wanted to improve his English, not that it needed any improvement apart from the odd explanation of an idiom. She only wished her Greek was half as good as his English. She was trying to pick up a few phrases, especially being surrounded by the Greek women at the factory all day, who no doubt talked about her rather than to her. She smiled as she recalled the faux pas she had already made with the language. In the first few weeks Zoe and Damianos had taken a trip up to the mountains on his motorbike where they had met his friend who owned a roadside taverna, half way up. It seemed as though no small trip could be complete for Cretans without meeting someone they knew. Zoe had

A Lock up on Crete

been introduced to his friend who had asked her if she worked in Iraepetra. At first, Zoe didn't know whether to divulge the information to a stranger, so she looked at Damianos who nodded. She was eager to speak a little Greek:

'Thoolevo sto ergostavio agori' Zoe was bemused when the taverna owner hid his face with his hand while his shoulders shuddered up and down. Damianos smiled at his friend's reaction as he pulled Zoe closer to him in a reassuring embrace.

'Hey did I say something wrong?'

'A little yes,' his friend replied as he placed his hands on his hips. 'Hey, at least you try. Most tourists don't.'

Damianos stepped in and whispered in her ear.

'Thoolevo sto angouri ergostavio,' she repeated.

'Ahh, you work in a cucumber factory!' his friend confirmed.

Damianos explained that she had first said she worked in a boy factory.

'Well come on boys! Angouri and Agori are similar!'

'True, True,' Damianos and his friend replied with a slight hint of friendly sarcasm as they finished off their coffees and continued up the steep incline, passing the ubiquitous olive groves interspersed with the odd lemon tree.

Istanbul

The next morning, Zoe's body, especially her head, felt like a lead weight as Michalis knocked on their door on the way to breakfast.

A Lock up on Crete

'Damianos. I don't feel like eating. I have a headache. You go with Michalis and bring me back a piece of bread please,' she'd urged him as he leapt into his jeans, ready for another hearty day of shopping. He'd almost decided on which jackets he would buy to gain the most profit back home. He leaned down and kissed her on her forehead before reaching into his small day bag and placing two painkillers on the bedside table.

Damianos returned all fired up for his second day of shopping. All Zoe could think about was the pillow that she could hardly lift her head from; she yearned for silence and sleep.

Half an hour later Damianos, Michalis and Zoe returned to the cacophony of the Grand Bazaar as the hammer in her head continued to bang on her skull. An hour later they were still in the same small shop as she slumped in a leather chair and closed her eyes

'Zoe, Zoe. Wake up I have bought this leather jacket. We are going to another shopping area now,' Damianos urged as he snatched the large paper bag from the counter. Michalis helped her from the chair.

'Oy! what the hell!' Zoe shrieked as they exited the Grand Bazaar out on the pavement. She swung around to see a small Turkish boy smiling mischievously at her, after pinching her bottom.

Damianos and Michalis threw a coin his way as she looked on incredulously.

'It's the best thing we can do with us being Greek and in our position,' Michalis shrugged as Damianos hailed a taxi and Zoe caught sight of another little street urchin -

A Lock up on Crete

palms open and feet tucked under to look as if his lower legs were missing.

Back at the hotel, Zoe excused herself and returned to the room, forgoing on the inclusive lunch.
'Boys please I will be fine on my own. I need to sleep. If it makes you feel better you can inform reception to check up on me every now and again.'
'Ach! Why we would allow a Turk to know you were alone in your room?' Damianos huffed, shaking his head. Michalis returned from the corridor and introduced Maria to Zoe.
'Ahhh Zoi Zoi – Life Life,' said the miniscule older lady as she took Zoe's hand in hers. Michalis spoke in Greek to her, explaining that Zoe was going to sleep while they went to pick up their shopping. Maria was one of the coach party who had accompanied her younger sister but she too had had enough of shopping and had returned to the hotel. Michalis asked if she could periodically check on Zoe as she was in the opposite room. As Damianos gave Maria his key she nodded enthusiastically, rushed to her room, returned and plonked herself on the chair opposite Zoe with her embroidery on her lap.

It must have been the melodic click clack of the needles that sent Zoe into a fitful sleep as she only woke up when the boys returned to the room where Maria was softly snoring in the chair, embroidery still in her lap and the needles precariously hanging off the edge of the chair.

A Lock up on Crete

'Your hands,' Damianos said as Michalis woke Maria to thank her.

'My hands. What about my hands? Oh they're stiff!' Zoe tried to prise them open. Both hands were in a clenched fist position with blister type markings on her palms.

'Zoe, do your hands hurt?' asked a worried looking Michalis as Damianos returned from the bathroom with a damp cloth.

'No, not at all but I just can't open them.'

'That's weird,' Damianos agreed as he rifled through his bag of tablets. Zoe wasn't aware he needed so many tablets and wondered if he had mistakenly given her the wrong tablets before for her headache; she hadn't slept so soundly for ages.

Both boys spoke in rapid Greek to each other, none of which she could decipher. She began to feel worried, trying to follow the terse conversation as a few hand gestures were exchanged between the two friends.

'Where did you put the empty blister pack Zoe?' Damianos asked as he felt her temperature. Zoe searched around her bed before spotting it on the floor. She handed it over. She heard a sigh of relief from the two boys as they nodded in agreement.

'Okay, Zoe, so when we are back in Iraepetra we will see how your hands are then unless you would like to ask the coach driver if he knows anywhere in Istanbul,' Damianos explained, carefully stroking her hair.

'God no I'm not letting anyone near me from here. When do we travel back?'

'Tomorrow morning. So you try to sleep more and then you will be fit for the journey. I think it best you don't

A Lock up on Crete

come down to dinner. We will ask for a meal to bring up to you,' Michalis offered as he stroked the two day stubble on his chin.

'No, no, I don't want any of this food. Maybe just a few biscuits or a bread roll with jam will be plenty,' Zoe whispered as the boys became blurry and she relented to sleep.

The return coach journey was just about bearable until they approached the Greek border. Zoe wondered why the Greeks were treated like criminals from the border control even entering their own country. Damianos instructed Zoe to stand close to him and to shield her hands away from the customs officials in case they asked about why she couldn't open them fully. She felt drowsy still, even though she had slept for what seemed like an eternity. She suddenly became conscious of her hands and felt she was being singled out already, as although she could pass as a Greek female with her dark hair and darkish complexion, she couldn't speak the language. There was a lot of shouting as the males were instructed to leave the females and line up in a different area. Damianos rifled through his suitcase thrusting two leather jackets and a pair of leather trousers onto an unprepared Zoe.

'Please Zoe just put them in your case and if the customs ask, say they are yours,' Damianos urged as he was swiftly moved on to the other line. A female official eyed them suspiciously. Without causing too much of a commotion, Zoe tried desperately to fit them in her case which proved difficult with the immobility of her hands.

A Lock up on Crete

She ended up wearing one of the jackets which was far too big for her but at least covered her hands.

'These leather. Who are these for?' Zoe was directed to a metal table by the customs official and instructed to open her case.

'They are for me and I have bought the other jacket for my brother back in England' Zoe lied as beads of sweat formed on her forehead.

'Why then are you wearing the jacket? It does not fit you.'

'Oh, it's just because I got mixed up and I couldn't fit it in my case,' she smiled at the unsmiling official.

'Passport,' he demanded, holding out his hand.

Zoe drew breath as she witnessed the official writing something in the back of her passport.

'When you arrive in your own country you will have to show your customs the two leather jackets and the one pair of leather trousers.' She was just about to ask him what the Greek words meant when he ushered her on. Zoe was in no mood to speak to Damianos and decided not to show him her passport just yet. She might even confide in Michalis instead and ask him what the words the official had wrote in her beloved passport actually meant. But for now she just wanted to get back on the coach and sleep.

Thessaloniki, Northern Greece

The coach pulled up at a parking spot opposite the seafront of Thessaloniki. It was dawn but the city was

A Lock up on Crete

already buzzing with life. Zoe wrestled between getting off the coach for some fresh air and a walk along the elegant looking promenade or to stay put on the coach. She decided on the former as she didn't want to arouse suspicion of her growing concern about her hands and general well- being.

Every step she took was agonising as she attempted to walk beside the boys on the wide promenade. She couldn't stand up straight. Like her hands, her body was bent double and there was a searing pain in her right side above her hip.

'Katsi, katsi. Sorry I mean sit sit,' Damianos said as he helped her to a bench while Michalis raced back to the coach to get some water and painkillers for her.

'I'm not taking those tablets,' she urged as she gulped at the water. Her thirst was unquenchable and she felt dizzy. Michalis told them to stay put while he searched for a pharmacy for some different painkillers. At least they had a half hour break and different painkillers might just do the trick. She had ruled out appendicitis as she had already had that removed.

To add to her worries she was still mithered about Damianos current disposition. He seemed on edge all of the time and she still hadn't shown him her passport. What exactly was he up to with these leather jackets and were they a ruse for something else he might be importing back to Greece? Whatever the problem was, she just wanted it to be over and her health to return to normal. She wanted to be with Mel and Tia and even the old battle axes in the cucumber factories blaming her for rubbing mouldy cucumbers. The last thought at least

A Lock up on Crete

made her smile but did little to relieve the dagger in her side.

Michalis returned with more painkillers urging her to take two immediately and to let him know how she felt after ten minutes. The pharmacist had been reluctant to sell them to him as he had not seen the patient.

Back on the coach, she fell into a deep sleep with Michalis periodically checking her pulse while Damianos attempted to prise her lips open to take some water. The next time she opened her eyes they were approaching the capital city of Athens.

'Hey Zoe. How are you feeling,' Damianos asked in an unusually high pitched voice.

'How long have I been asleep?'

'At least seven hours. We are nearly in Athens. My sister, Ariadne lives here. Before we leave tomorrow night for Crete we will stay with her,' Damianos explained as he prepared to gather their belongings.

'She needs to go to hospital now,' Ariadne said first in Greek then in English for Zoe's benefit. 'Look at her! She is bent!' she continued as she ordered a taxi to the main hospital in the centre of Athens. 'I will come with you. Pah! Useless men,' she added.

Ushered into a disinfectant smelling cold room which could have doubled as the morgue, Zoe was laid out onto a bare marble slab as the fluorescent strip above flickered on and off. How could anyone concentrate with that buzzing noise above them, she thought.

'Hurt here?' the heavily bearded doctor asked as he prodded Zoe's side with his fingers.

A Lock up on Crete

'Just a bit,' she winced wondering if he really was the best surgeon in the whole of Athens as recommended by Ariadne.

'What you mean. Just? Does it hurt, yes, or does it hurt, no? Does it hurt little or much,' he bawled as he attempted to prise open her hands.

'Ouch, yes it hurts. My hands hurt more,' she added. He did not reply, instead turning to Damianos and his sister in a gabble of Greek.

'Ella, ella, sico pano,' Ariadne comforted Zoe as the surgeon left the room with Damianos to sort out the fee. Ariadne whose beautiful face and flawless skin Zoe couldn't help admiring, carefully and discreetly helped her out of her hospital gown.

'The doctor is a friend of my friend from university and although he is a bit how you say, bossy, I do trust his word. As you have already had your appendix removed he thinks it could have been a virus from your trip to Turkey. It could be anything from the air con in the coach or hotel. But because you didn't jump to the ceiling when he touched your side he advises to check with the doctor in Iraepetra. However, if you like, you can stay with me here in Athens until you feel better. The only problem is the money for the fees unless you have some already.' Ariadne explained with a hint of embarrassment reflected in her eyes.

'I need to go to the bank for the money. Do they need it straight away?'

'Yes they do. But wait. I can tell my brother to pay with his money and then you can pay him back.' Zoe thanked her as she rushed out and banged the door hard.

A Lock up on Crete

'It is all paid for now. Do not worry. I am a Greek and it is my duty as a Greek to show filoxenia (kindness to strangers) and you seem to make my brother smile and he also seems to have plenty of money so that is a good sign. If it makes you feel good you can buy me a drink or two when I come to visit my parents in Iraepetra next month. I haven't seen them for about six months.'

Zoe noticed her slight bump and wondered what her back story was. Maybe she would find out soon.

Zoe hoped that with Michalis already on the ferry back to Crete, having had to get back to work, Damianos might decide to spend some time with his sister. It felt good to have another female to be around, especially one so level headed as Ariadne portrayed. However, Zoe knew that it would probably be better to get back to Crete as she had her health card registered there and she couldn't possibly be able to afford the Athens doctor again. Damianos hadn't even mentioned the fee he had paid.

After another good sleep, but reluctant to leave the comfort of Ariadne's spotless Athenian apartment, they said their farewells and took the short taxi ride to the port of Piraeus where they boarded the ferry to Crete. She felt much older than her years as she hobbled on to the gangplank while Damianos carried both cases. She made sure her passport was tucked away safely in her travel pouch which she kept close to her chest under her clothes. She just needed her own mother now and if her health didn't improve soon she may be seeing her sooner than later.

A Lock up on Crete

Chapter 6

Mel and Yannis

Yannis had heard that Mel, the English girl whom he had made friends with four years previously, had been spotted back in Iraepetra. Apparently, she was had arrived with two other young women and had started working, becoming quite well known for her English puddings and pastries. Yannis assumed that she was still working illegally. Mel with the fiery red curls had been vivacious and fun to be around. But that was four years ago when he had been an electrician's apprentice. Four years on and he had somehow made his way into the Ministry of Defence as an advisor concerning electrical contracts. Consequently he had signed the official Secret Act. Although he quite liked the mystery surrounding his title, it had become tedious when he visited home. His friends and acquaintances had started to buy him drinks at the bar and he was sure they sometimes spiked them in an attempt to loosen his lips and reveal the secrets. For that reason he made sure he declined the offer of alcohol when he was back home in Iraepetra. Although he loved his friends and family dearly he also loved his job and the comfort and perks that came with it. In fact he was due a few days leave and although he was based in Cyprus it was easy enough to fly from Paphos to Sitia at the tip of Eastern Crete. Another bonus with his work was the all- expenses paid taxi that would be waiting for him at the small city airport to deliver him back home.

A Lock up on Crete

This trip home would be even more special as he had a considerable amount of money he had saved up to deposit in his parents bank account. They had struggled for so many years after the extortionate amount of money they had wasted on bailing out his younger, good for nothing brother, who had been imprisoned in the infamous jail of Neapoli. He remembered the day that he was sentenced and his poor parents having to face the humiliation in the huge, austere court room which juxtaposed ironically with the elegant main church of Neapoli. Yannis also cast his mind back and shuddered when he had seen the prison rising beyond the church, a mere 100 metres from the national road. It had obviously been built before the new national road and it almost screamed out a warning to drivers and their passengers not to mess with the law. Fortunately, for his younger wayward brother, he only spent one night in jail as his parents had released the family savings to bail him out. He and his relatives had been livid, knowing how his parents had lived in near poverty all their lives. He recalled aunt Apollonia screaming at the judge to be lenient with his sentence; she was duly removed from the court house and loitered outside in the burning sun while the jury decided the fate of her nephew. Yannis couldn't remember much about what had happened after that – all he knew was he was even more determined to find a well- paid job and return his parents hard earned savings on behalf of his younger brother.

Four years previously

A Lock up on Crete

Mel and Yannis, Iraepetra 1980

A few months later in the autumn of 1980 Melissa or
Mel as she preferred, entered his life. The few winter
months they had spent together in Iraepetra had been
his happiest. Always shy with the girls, she had instilled
confidence and a passion for life into him. Despite what
most people thought, their relationship was purely
platonic. At the time he was managing one of the olive
oil factories for a few families and was in charge of
finding the labour to harvest the crops. It had been
difficult to find willing locals and he too had to resort to
employing the few illegal touristees in order to get the
olives picked as the timing was crucial. That was the first
time he had seen her. She had been making toasties in
the kitchen at Fotis's café bar when she smiled at him
through the serving hatch. Within an hour he had
poached her for a few days from Fotis who understood
Yannis's dilemma with harvesting the olives.

 Mel started the very next day with a few more
touristees. He remembered when he had handed each
of them a wand like stick.

'Tools of the trade eh?' Mel had asked with a grin that lit
up the unusually dull day (Iraepetra received the most
sunshine on the whole of the island due to its southerly
location looking out onto the Libyan sea.) The two Kiwi
touristees also looked at the stick then to each other,
then to Yannis for clarification.

'Ella, come, I will show you,' Yannis smiled as he led
them to a clearing in the olive grove where he had
prepared the area to harvest. The three new workers
stood around the clearing. The ground in between the

A Lock up on Crete

trees was covered with a faded green tarpaulin and three short wooden ladders had been erected in the nearby trees. At the side of the tarp stood threadbare sacks, waiting to be filled with olives. An old rusty wheelbarrow sat between them.

'So is this what we use to take the olives off the trees Yannis?' the ginger Kiwi male asked, who looked to be desperately trying to grow a winter beard but without much success.

'Ne, ne, yes, yes. It does look a little ancient but if you wear these gloves you will have no problem. This family who owns these trees do not have an electric machine and that is why you are employed along with the stick.' Yannis left them to it saying that he needed to start up the press machine and that he would return in an hour. The other kiwi was a waif like female with freckles and bunches in her hair.

'Well I guess we'd better give it a go then,' chimed Mel as she aimed the stick at a bountiful branch, straining under its own weight with sage green olives. With a few whacks from the stick, the olives surrendered their hold on the branch and thudded to the ground. By noon, Yannis had still not returned but his three workers had already bagged a few sacks of olives and sat them in the wheelbarrows, ready for the press.

Yannis eventually returned with a souvlaki stick and salad for his three ravenous workers. They didn't realise just how hungry they were as they devoured the herby meat and super fresh salad of beef tomatoes, cucumber and the ubiquitous Feta cheese.

A Lock up on Crete

'Bravo, bravo!' Yannis whooped as he looked around the clearing. 'Fantastic work girls and boy. I want you back tomorrow.' He gave Mel a sneaky wink. She blushed as he had done when she had smiled at him the first time they had met.

Near the end of their long day, Mel regretted not wearing the gloves that Yannis had provided. She had a bit of a silly phobia about gloves stemming from her childhood when a stupid clown at a summer fete had smothered her face with his gigantic clown glove. She looked at her hands. They were red raw. She winced as she popped a few blisters making sure she hid them from Yannis as she wanted to come back the next day. It had been liberating being in the fresh air all day as opposed to a kitchen and was already looking forward to the next day.

After securing the equipment between the olive trees, Yannis gave them a lift back into town in his pick- up truck. Mel loved it in these open trucks. Even the simplistic way they could travel in the open back without freezing was liberating. She tittered as she imagined doing the same back home. As she bid the two Kiwis good night, Yannis gestured for her to go over to him.'

'Tomorrow you must wear the gloves I provided. I saw your blisters and they are not good. I do not want to be blamed for mistreating my staff when Fotis has been good enough to loan you to me. Now please here is some money for the pharmacy. I will see you same time and same place in the morning.'

Present day 1984

A Lock up on Crete

Yannis was now back in his hometown and as usual he hadn't told anyone; it was easier that way. He asked the taxi driver to stop outside Fotis's café bar to see his good friend and to pay him a debt that was long overdue or maybe it was more like compensation. He made his way from the main road that ran parallel to the seafront, glancing around him as he did so. On the other side of the road, Mel was on her way back to the apartment from her shift at Medusa restaurant. She froze for a fleeting moment as the side profile of a familiar figure stepped out of a taxi. It was later that evening when it clicked. She continued on her way when she bumped into Zoe and Damianos coming out of the pharmacy, laden with a few pharmacy bags.

'Hey, look who is back in town then,' she exclaimed as Mel went in for a bear hug. Zoe winced in pain as Damianos explained the reason for being in the pharmacy.

'Jeez, Zoe, you look like you've lost weight too. Are you coming back to the apartment?'

'I'm staying with Damianos's aunty who has a spare room. She lives next door to his parents and she said she will look after me for a few days while Damianos and his mother go back to the factory. And I knew you would be busy too so I accepted the offer. I'm so tired all the time. I'm going to the apartment for some clothes but I really need to sleep soon.'

'I'll come with you. I was just about to go to the pharmacy myself but it can wait. Actually, do you fancy a cappuchino at Fotis's?'

A Lock up on Crete

Both girls were glad to be in each other's company as they sat outside in the comfy bucket chairs.

'Where's Tia by the way,' Zoe asked. Mel explained that Tia and Andreas had gone to his family up in Vai where his uncle needed some help planting some palm trees.

'Sounds exotic,' Zoe replied as they both nodded and waited for their coffees.

Damianos returned from speaking with Fotis inside the café with a huge surprise for Mel.

'Oh my God! It is you Yannis. Ti kanis -How are you?' Mel shrilled as she rose from her seat and flung her arms around him.

'Good to see you Meli mou. You haven't changed one little bit. A little birdy told me you were back in town,' (an expression Mel had taught him before.)

Zoe's eyes were closing rapidly as Damianos explained that they needed to go. Yannis and Mel or Meli mou as he called her, it seemed, had quite a lot of catching up to do.

An hour later, Katerina, dressed in her black widow weeds welcomed her favourite nephew and girlfriend. She spoke a little English as she showed Zoe to a comfortable airy bedroom with a double bed in the middle, facing a window. There was a sink in the corner and even a little fridge. The bed seemed to come alive, pulling her into its embrace. Following Katerina's instructions, Damianos kissed Zoe good night telling her he would call on her after work the next day. Zoe was left to sleep being comforted by the knowledge that Damianos would be sleeping in his bedroom only a few metres away over the low fence that separated his house from his aunts. Katerina was also nearby in the adjacent bedroom. Zoe promptly fell asleep allowing her medication to do its magic.

Chapter 7

Tia and Andreas – Vai beach

Andreas gently stirred the sleeping Tia. He smiled at the way she wore a hairnet in bed. He was pleased she took great care of her appearance. Not that the local girls in Iraepetra didn't but with Tia, she seemed to have a keen eye on how to accessorise her outfits and her hair was her crowning glory, always meticulous. He wondered, as he noticed a few curls that escaped the hairnet, whether it was naturally curly and naturally dark brown in colour. He made a note to himself not to ask her just yet. Maybe once they had gotten past that initial stage. Growing up with three sisters had shaped his knowledge on the right and not so right questions to ask the female species. As Tia stirred, he felt his heart flutter and knew at that moment he wanted her to be his wife. Andreas had had a few lasting relationships with the local girls but he hadn't felt that thunderbolt like he had outside the toilets of Zeus bar with Tia. He only hoped she felt the same way.

Tia dressed in a simple summer dress with a matching headscarf as the south east of Crete was having a winter

A Lock up on Crete

heatwave. It felt good again for her body to be caressed by the warm winter sun. The last few weeks had been too cold for her and the apartment with the tiled floors, bare plastered walls and no heating. Even the bars that they frequented at night and the tavernas they had most of their evening meals in, didn't seem to be geared up for the colder weather. After a few days where she had no work, she had resorted to leaving the two ring hob on all day while sat in the apartment on her own twiddling her thumbs. It was only when they received a visit from Theo, with a higher than average electric bill, did she go to sleep with a few more layers of clothing on and made sure she looked for work.

As she stepped out onto the patio of Andreas's uncle's home, nestled at the top of the palm grove plantation, she stopped to take in the sheer beauty of her surroundings. From their elevation, she could see the sea as it gently lapped the palm fringed beach. She felt a bit silly imagining herself in a Bounty advert, reaching out for the bar of coconut chocolate.

'Kalimera agape mou,' (good morning my love), Andreas greeted her as he placed a tray of coffee and toast on the patio table. He had got the hang of making toast with butter and jam for Tia now and had even ordered a toaster from the local hardware shop. Breakfasting on the patio with the idyllic view and unseasonal good weather, Andreas wished they could have just lazed the few days away instead of the manual work of planting baby palms they were about to start. Seeing Tia in her summer dress and little red heeled shoes, he felt

A Lock up on Crete

embarrassed that, after breakfast, they really needed to be cracking on with planting the palm seedlings while they were blessed with the weather. If only they could capture this moment and make it last all day. Then, by a stroke of luck his wish was fulfilled as a horn blasted from the road above the house. He went out via the side path to investigate.

'Andreas, Andreas, is that you?' The voice was vaguely familiar but he couldn't quite put a name to it until he saw his cousin in his utility truck.

'Kalimera, kalimera Andreas. Papa says not to start the work today. He is still in Sitia waiting for the plants. They were supposed to be here this morning on the ferry but have been delayed. Have a nice day with your English touristee,' he said, winking at his cousin before kicking up some gravel with his tyres.

The sea was cool but bearable as they walked hand in hand the full length of the deserted beach. On the two hour journey from Iraepetra, they had stopped for a break at the small seaside resort of Makry Gialos. Although it looked like a nice little resort during the summer, in November it seemed to be grieving at the lack of life and tourists. Tavernas and bars were boarded up ready for the winter storms and a few stray beach umbrellas had made their escape to the sea, trapped under the wooden structure of a beachfront restaurant. Driving north from Makry Gialos they had arrived in the city of Sitia. Andreas had popped into his uncle's office to pick up the key to the house in Vai. Tia liked the atmosphere here in this picturesque coastal city. There

A Lock up on Crete

was more of a buzz about it and although not as cosmopolitan as Agios Nikolaos, of which she would like to return to soon, Sitia was more of a fishing town but also with a pleasant promenade and even had an airport very close on the outskirts of town.

Tia knew that this day would be one of those extra special days where her memory would return to often. She wanted time to stop still. To their delight, they had discovered that Andreas's uncle had stocked the fridge with a substantial supply of meat, vegetables, cheese and beers. Thus, Andreas prepared lunch while Tia changed her outfit. She was glad that she had brought along the long white dress she had treated herself to in Iraepetra in the autumn sales. She was disappointed she didn't have shoes to match so she slipped on her flip flops. She sauntered onto the patio feeling an overwhelming sense of wellbeing. She knew there and then that the Cretan soul –'psyche' had truly captured her. For some uncanny reason, she truly felt she was at home where she was meant to be. And although she adored her family and roots in Scotland, she just couldn't help feel the pull of this magnetic island. She always knew deep down that she would relocate somewhere warmer than her birth country. Growing up, she had always been the kid with the multitude of jumpers on – constantly shivering, even in the summer. Maybe she had inherited her grandfather's Italian blood. Happy memories returned as she visualised herself as a little girl again holding her dear grandfather's hand who would lead her into the small ice cream factory just outside of Glasgow. With his full head of white hair he would don his hairnet and striped apron and attempt to show her how to make the real ice cream – Italian ice cream.

The small factory had been passed to her father who unfortunately was sick of the sight of ice cream and subsequently sold it to fund the bespoke building of their luxurious family home. Hopefully Grandpapa Giovanni would have approved from his grave in the knowledge that the fruits of his labour, from humble beginnings in an impoverished area of Italy, and his brave decision to emigrate to Scotland armed with just his skills in the art of ice cream, had benefitted his son and family with a beautiful home and comfortable lifestyle.

'Hey, penny for your thought, agape mou,' Andreas said as he laid the lunch on the table.

'Oh I'm just thinking about my grandpapa Giovanni,' Tia answered, placing a napkin on her lap.

'Oh I didn't know you had Italian blood, although you do have more Mediterranean looks that English. I thought that when we first met.'

'Scottish not English!' Tia reminded him with a mocking stare.

'Oh of course you little Scottish lady,' he grinned. 'But then why did your parents give you a Greek name? Tia means Goddess in Greek!' he added. 'Tia, my Greek/Italian goddess.' Andreas teased as he opened two cold beers. Tia reflected on the name she had been given and felt far more of a connection here in Greece than the numerous visits to Italy, visiting Grandpapa Giovanni. Maybe his relatives down the line had

A Lock up on Crete

originally been Greek and made their way to Italy and settled or maybe, although it was her first time on Greek soil, it was the uniqueness of Crete that made her feel so at home. Her mind wandered off to Chris the ex who she had rarely thought about except when he popped up in an unwelcome dream. On reflection, the cause of her breaking off their engagement might not have been entirely his fault: even with the luxurious lifestyle that they would doubt have had, would she honestly have ever been content? Tia knew that deep down, she had always pined for somewhere like this to live her life and now she had found it, with the added bonus of meeting the warm hearted soul that was Andreas, she wasn't letting it go.

Mel and Yannis, present day, Iraepetra

'So how long are you in town for Yannis?'

'Four days, Meli mou. Maybe we could take a trip somewhere together? I will tell your boss tomorrow to allow you a few days off,' Yannis suggested as he gazed into her striking green eyes.

'Yannis, you can't just demand I have time off. I'm a busy baking lady - baking, baking and more baking,' she teased as she instinctively looped her arm around his. The next day Yannis strolled into the Medusa restaurant and after an animated conversation with Mel's boss, crept up behind Mel as she sprinkled desiccated coconut over a cake and unfastened her apron.

'Whoaaa!' she shrieked as she spun around, spraying tiny white flakes into the air.

A Lock up on Crete

By noon they were well on their way west, hugging the coastline. Yannis was glad to be back on his powerful motorbike that he stored at his parents' house. As Mel snuggled into his back, Yannis reflected on how good it had been the day before. The moment he met up with Meli again, his confidence went through the roof. How did she do it? Even with his prominent position at work, he still doubted himself and his sexuality. He had never had a proper girlfriend, much to the chagrin of his Aunt Apollonia, who kept on and on at him – she had even resorted to writing to him in Cyprus asking if he had met a nice village Cypriot girl yet. *You must marry soon Yannis. Don't leave it too late like I did and be without a good man and children. It is very lonely.* He recalled reading her small scribble in the mail he received which had to be first read by his superiors. Thankfully Aunt Apollonia, who had moved to Agios Nikolaos many years ago, was too far away when he presented his parents with the generous cheque to compensate for his brother's misdemeanours.

Tears to fill a bucket had streamed down both his mama and papa's eyes as they hugged their caring son. Years of scrimping and relying on food banks, which they had managed to keep secret, had been washed away with their tears. Yannis assured them he had not left himself short and it was the least he could do, adding that he was very happy with his job and living in Cyprus. He loved his parents so much: they were gentle people and didn't thrive on gossip, unlike his aunt Apollonia; no wonder she had never married he thought.

A Lock up on Crete

Sat down, in the humble yard, with a few potted herb plants and a stray bougainvillea climbing up the wall, he had enquired about his wayward brother's whereabouts. His elderly papa shrugged his broad shoulders and his mama had hobbled off to the humble kitchen, returning with a plateful of the best meatballs in the whole of Crete.

He snapped out of his reverie as they approached the former hippy hang out of Matala in the late afternoon. The sandstone cliffs and the caves, inhabited in the 1960's by the hippies, reached out to the sea, shielding the deserted beach from the late November wind. Luckily, there were a few small guest houses still open as they locked up the bike and settled in for the night. That night, Yannis attempted to teach Mel how to play backgammon while they were entertained by the owner's children - who were glad of some visitors to show off their dancing and acrobatic skills to.

After breakfast the next morning, they continued on their ride west. Mel had a good eye for directions and was confused when Yannis turned right instead of left, following a narrow track that meandered down to cliffs. 'I forgot to stop here on the way yesterday,' he explained as they came to a sign saying Kokkino Amos – red beach. After securing the motorbike, they descended the steep steps to another deserted beach.

'You should see this beach in summer – jam packed as you English say. I don't know why you have all these funny words for describing things but I like them.'

Mel imagined the hordes of tourists competing for a sunbed and was glad they could witness the orangey red

A Lock up on Crete

sand alone as she skimmed a pebble into the calm sea, watching it bounce away into a watery grave.

'Hey Meli mou, I like your skills. You are not just a crazy red headed baker, are you?'

'I am what they say in English – jack of all trades, master of none.' She continued skimming, leaving Yannis to mull over the latest idiom.

They continued their journey west passing Tympaki with a landscape of plastic greenhouses similar to Iraepetra.

'Meli mou?' Yannis pulled up to the heavily secured fence and took his helmet off. 'This is Timpaki airport. It was built by the Germans in 1941 during World War 2. It was mainly used with resupplying German operations in North Africa but now belongs to Greece and is used by the Air force as a military base.'

'You really are a wealth of information Yannis Pavlavakis,' Mel resisted asking for more information, taking into account his current occupation in Cyprus and the need to say less rather than more. She wondered how it would be to sign the official Secrets Act. She didn't think she would be able to do it. Whenever someone asked her to keep a secret, she flatly refused.

An hour's ride later they spotted signs for Preveli Lake and a heavily pitted roadside sign of people hiking. Mel, desperate for some exercise to alleviate her numb bum, tapped Yannis on the shoulder indicating to pull over.

'Yannis, could we spend a little while here and maybe have a walk. It looks stunning.'

'Of course Meli mou, I want to show you the very best of my beautiful island.' He continued to ride around the

A Lock up on Crete

gorge and further down until they reached a deserted car park.

'Oh my Lord,' Mel exclaimed as she climbed off the large shiny black beast of a bike.

'Have we arrived in paradise?' she said out loud as Yannis secured the motorbike.

Mel looked upwards - she could make out a gorge which filtered into a palm fringed lake which in turn filtered onto the beach and finally meandered into the turquoise sea. The whole area was unlike anywhere she had ever been.

'Well actually it is what you call irony that it looks like paradise as this is the beach where thousands of Allied troops were evacuated from when the Germans took over the island in WW2. I imagine the tired and defeated soldiers were relieved to be rescued but sad to have to leave the paradise behind to the Germans.' Yannis bowed his head and crossed himself as Mel replicated his actions.

They walked the short gradient to the top of the lake then down to the beach, dipping in and out of the line of palm trees whose fronds swayed like welcoming arms, guiding them downwards.

'If it was summer I would be stripping off and jumping in that water with you.' Mel cringed as she said the words, realising this was not the time or place to be making flippant remarks like that. Yannis didn't respond and she hoped he hadn't paid attention to her words. She wondered how unlike a typical young Greek he was – almost the opposite of the Greek Kamaki of which they were plenty, even in Iraepetra. She had first heard of the

A Lock up on Crete

term four years previously. She recalled an elderly Greek woman reciting the meaning in perfect English to her. *'A kamaki is a young Greek who devotes his summers to conquering as many foreign, pretty women he can. He then returns to his gang of male friends to boast about his conquests. Kamaki translates to harpoon.'* It was as if the dear old lady made it her duty to forewarn the female foreigners who visited Iraepetra to save any heartache and also to keep the menfolk engaged more with the local Greek girls.

They were amazed to find that the taverna which hugged the steep cliff down to the beach was open. Suddenly starving they sat down and ordered a fish lunch. Just as their food arrived, so did a large party of adults and children. They were soon sat eating their lunch in the middle of an extended family, celebrating Yiayia's 80th birthday.

'Why did the staff allow us to eat here when they knew they had a private party booked?' Mel whispered to Yannis as she devoured the lemon potatoes and fresh fish.

'Why would they not?' he answered again with a puzzled look. 'If someone is already in the restaurant then they are welcome too. We would not think to make people feel uncomfortable.'

Mel reasoned with his answer, musing how different their cultures were in this respect. She watched in awe as the extended family seated themselves, making sure the children sat amongst the adults, young and old alike. She was taken aback when a pretty young girl handed her a posy of dried flowers.

A Lock up on Crete

'Efcharsto poli,' Mel thanked her in Greek, 'poly omorfi,'
(very beautiful) The young girl almost curtsied before
she skipped back to her Yiayia (Grandma)

'Yannis I don't want to leave this paradise,' Mel
announced as the waiter brought them a carafe of house
wine, courtesy of the octogenarian Yiayia who raised her
glass to them from the far side of the room.
'You see the kindness to strangers 'filoxenia' extends to
Greeks also, not only to you tourists,' Yannis explained
as Mel shook her head slightly in wonderment. One
more carafe later, Yannis decided to treat Mel to the
Cretan Sirtaki (Zorba the Greek) on the makeshift dance
floor. A group of giggling girls pulled at Mel's hand,
urging her to join them as they responded to the males
and formed a circle around them. Mel loved the
spontaneity of it all and was in her element when she
caught sight of Yannis being whirled around the middle
of the circle by the very nimble Yiayia. She also noted the
young Greek guy rescue him with a warm embrace. The
night became hazy around the edges and the last thing
Mel remembered was tucking into a mattress on the
floor and pulling a thin blanket over her.

It was six am in the morning when Mel awoke with a
raging thirst. Luckily someone, probably the person who
had put her to bed, had left a bottle of water on the
floor beside her makeshift bed. Her neck ached as she
turned around to take in her surroundings. Yannis was
fast asleep in another makeshift bed a few metres to the
right, his dark curls contrasting with the white pillow. It

A Lock up on Crete

looked obvious that her male friend was a hit with the local females too as the back of a head with dark curls, a little longer than Yannis', lay next to him.

 She felt a little awkward at the sight of her good friend snuggled up to his one night stand - she averted her eyes as the sheet fell below his waist, revealing his tanned, toned buttocks.

In those fleeting moments between wanting to stare longer than she ought, she thought she saw a tattoo at the top of Yannis' buttocks as he wriggled and moved closer to his new friend. Where had she seen a tattoo like that and in the same place she wondered as she gingerly moved her weary body form the floor.

Mini hammers knocked on her skull as she dressed and traversed the floor which was scattered with mattresses and all ages of party revellers still deep in the throes of sleep. She wrapped her cardigan around her and descended the spiral staircase into the kitchen below. The taverna owner recognised her plight and sat her down at a table.

'Ahh you head aches?'

'Just a bit yes. Efcharisto for the tablets,' Mel replied as she wished she hadn't drunk so much.

Half an hour later, looking just ever so slightly sheepish, Yannis joined Mel on the terrace overlooking the beach.

'Beautiful view, hey Yannis?'

'Yes, my island is full of amazing views and now I think we should make our way inland. There are many more beautiful beaches west of here but unfortunately we don't have the time so I have a few friends in Heraklion I

A Lock up on Crete

would like you to meet. What do you say Meli mou?' If Yannis was embarrassed from his close encounter with the male from the night before, he sure didn't show it, Mel thought.

'I can't believe, even when we first met four years ago, that I didn't explore more of your wonderful and diverse island. These few days have been amazing and I would love to go into the mountains. But I do have a question for you Yannis. You don't have to answer but sometimes I wonder why you treat me like this and want to spend your precious time with me. Surely you have other friends and family you need to catch up with? Maybe some male friends?' she knew he knew what she was angling for.

'Like you say, you don't expect an answer,' he replied as they made their way to the car park.

Yannis felt at peace on his motorbike as he negotiated the narrow tracks up from the coast and into the interior of his beloved Crete. He also liked Cyprus and had a smaller motorbike there. On his days off he would ride around the island, mindful not to ride near the border of the Turkish territory. And although Cyprus was still Greece, some things were just not like Crete. With the British influence and a large community of ex pats, he didn't feel the same culture and traditions. Maybe he would finish his two year appointment early and return home. If not Iraepetra, he could make a home somewhere else on the island. He would gauge how Heraklion was like in the winter months and maybe he could relocate there and buy a nice house on the outskirts. He had options and was his own free person

A Lock up on Crete

with no one telling him what to do and that made him feel content.

As the track merged onto the National road he was able to increase speed, aware he was riding with pillion. When he made a quick decision to detour, turning off the main highway a little too abruptly, he felt the force of Mel's ample chest in the hollow of his back. Although Mel was an extremely attractive woman, there was no sexual attraction on his part. His mind wandered back to the amorous male he had woken up next to. He couldn't quite come to terms with his sexual deviances and sometimes wished he did have sexual feelings for Mel but at this moment in time he was just very grateful that they were spending quality time together. He felt proud that he could show her some of Crete's best kept treasures as they drove towards Phaistos, known for its Minoan Palace excavations.

As the two good friends wandered around the amazing archaeological site arm in arm, the only sound around them was a strange bleeting.

'Meli mou, quick, look, but don't move,' Yannis pulled her down to the gravel.

Before them, just a few metres away were a small family of goats, also wandering around as though they were enjoying the great Minoan archaeological site.

'These are the wild Kri Kri goats or sometimes they are called ibex. They are usually found more west from here near the White Mountains.' Yannis whispered.

'Maybe they are not the wild goats then,' Mel offered.

'No! they are Kri Kri. I can tell by their colouring.' Mel sensed a tinge of annoyance in his voice as the goats disappeared from view into the shrubbery.

Back on the national road, Mel looked forward to reaching Heraklion. She had worked there for a spell on her previous visit. It had been a crazy time she recalled:

Four years previously – Heraklion, September 1980

Mel and Rosie

Mel recalled her time with Rosie: Rosie's sister had worked in Iraepetra the year before and had prompted her younger sister Rosie to visit on her gap year from university. On numerous occasions her sister had boasted about her male conquests. Rosie wasn't so interested in searching for a Greek suitor. Rosie was more interested in exploring the rich history of Crete. She was particularly interested in the World War 2, Battle of Crete that she had chosen to do her dissertation on it.

Most of the time, Mel had worked in Ierapetra while Rosie had ventured off on her own exploring the main War memorials located all over Crete. She had been as far as Chania and Souda Bay on the north -west side of the island, taking photographs and journalling interviews she had conducted with the local people, most of whom had been through the torture. However, by early October, funds needed replenishing so they travelled to Heraklion in the hope they would find work on the grape harvest.

A Lock up on Crete

Their first priority was somewhere to live. Heraklion seemed like another world away from the sleepy villages of southern Crete. As they walked up from the main bus station, Rosie spotted a large guest house on the corner of a busy roundabout. Within minutes the two girls were offered a job in the pension as it was named, which was run by a tall Dutch lady and her Greek husband. The girls were to clean the rooms and generally man the reception when Spiro and Eva were out.

There was something quite refreshing about being a twenty year old in the fact that not a lot generally fazes you. However, on this occasion Rosie and Mel were lost for words when Eva showed them to their room.

'Here is your room. It is small but I think you will be comfortable and if we have a spare room in the dormitory you can have a bed but you must vacate the bed in the night if we receive a paying guest,' Eva explained, as though it was quite a normal arrangement. 'It's ok we will be good here,' assured Rosie, thankful that they at least had their lodgings sorted.

Mel stayed silent after spotting the faded 'Dangerous Chemicals' sign hanging on the door. As if they were going to sleep within inches of each other in a cleaning cupboard with a double mattress occupying all the space! It could be worse Mel thought to herself – she had slept on numerous roofs of hostels in Greece before now - although that wouldn't be a bad idea especially if either of them snored or the broom cupboard became a sauna.

By day two it was evident that there was only enough work for one of them at the pension. Eva told them

A Lock up on Crete

where to go to ask for working on the grapes. Just a short walk away they found the taverna where the manager, known amongst the transient workers simply as Avroti (farmer), usually put them in contact with trusted farmers. They decided that they would keep both the job at the pension and the grapes and work it between them alternatively.

The girls tossed a coin to decide who would work on the grapes first. As Mel ordered a coffee with the waitress she was handed a name and telephone number for work.

After a difficult half Greek half English conversation with a farmer named Stelios, Mel waited outside the taverna in the early morning sunshine for her employer. Stelios a middle aged man with a wiry moustache pulled up.

'Meli? Meli? Work with grapes?' it seemed like the name Meli meaning 'honey' in Greek, was now beginning to stick but she'd been called worse she tittered to herself.

'Ti simveni?' Stelios asked with a furrowed brow.

'No nothing is wrong Stelios. Ine kalo – it's good,' she assured him as she hauled herself into the tattered passenger seat. Soon they were driving up to the foothills overlooking the white city of Heraklion. It was good to be on top of the city looking down to the ever turquoise sea, interspersed with large ferries and smaller fishing boats.

One by one, Stelios' workforce introduced themselves to Mel. A female, probably much younger than she actually looked, who spoke good English, shook her hand so hard it made her wince.

A Lock up on Crete

'I am Maria Ladakis and I believe those two boys are from Thessaloniki, a big city in the north. They tipped their black caps to Mel like older men might have. However, from their tanned round faces, they could have only been leaving their teens. Lastly, an older lady with a toothless smile introduced herself simply as Yiayia. Just whose grandma she was, was anyone's guess but she looked like she was in the middle of preparing lunch, so that was a bonus.

Mel's first day picking grapes had been progressing well. The grape vines were actually low shrubs, so although she spent many hours crouched down, the plump grapes literally fell into her hands with the slightest touch. She was fast filling bucket after bucket loads much to the pleasure of Stelios who patrolled the rows of grapes with a knotted hankie over his head and an unlit cigarette perched in the corner of his mouth.
Lunch was served by Yiayia and was, as assumed, simply delicious. All the usual fresh local produce was laid out in a clearing at the top of the vineyard as everyone fell silent to concentrate on the bountiful food. Feeling quite full and very sleepy, Mel returned to work. The late September sunshine warmed her body and gave her the energy to carry on until she heard some commotion from up above. She was used to the Greeks shouting at each other but this sounded like a crazed person had broken free from an institution. Maria threw her bucket down to the ground as black grapes shot through the air like pellets. She then gave Stelios the flat palm gesture before ordering Yiayia to collect her belongings. Maria

A Lock up on Crete

Ladakis accompanied by Yiayia drove off on a battered scooter, with Yiayia riding side pillion as she clutched on to her baskets of food. Next, the two boys followed suit and drove off in what must have been their battered pickup. Stelios looked over at Mel, shrugged his shoulders and proceeded to empty the plump grapes onto the netting where they would eventually dry to become sultanas or raisins.

'So how was your first day,' Rosie asked as Mel returned the cleaning bucket into their broom cupboard.
'Eventful to say the least!'
'Oh same as mine then,' Rosie replied, locking their broom cupboard behind them as they went in search of something to eat.
'So I cleaned all the dormitories and toilets and then Eva took me on the roof to show me the water tanks. She said they would be out all afternoon and at 2pm the water would be coming through. I had to sit on the roof to open the valves and then turn them off when the two tanks were full, which I did. So then, when they returned at four o clock, Eva came down to the broom cupboard where I was having a quick snooze and played holy hell with me,' Rosie explained as she paused for breath.
'What had you done so wrong then?'
'She said I had turned the valve off too soon and I should have let the water fill right up to the brim and that now they would be a whole day without water. Apparently they can only fill it up every week.'

A Lock up on Crete

'Well that's her fault for not explaining it properly. She could quite easily have put a marker pen on where to fill it to.'
Both girls couldn't decide what they wanted to eat so settled for a carafe of wine accompanied by small saucers of nuts and olives instead. After polishing off another carafe they both felt in better spirits, laughing about their respective first day's work.

One month went by where they slipped into a successful routine of taking it in turns to work at the pension and the other day with the grape harvest. After the last of the dried grapes had been bagged up, it was with a heavy heart that the girls said goodbye to their employers and vacated their broom cupboard. They left Crete that afternoon on a ferry bound for Athens - the next stage of their adventure.

Mel and Yannis, Heraklion, present day
Four years on from her adventures with Rosie, Mel was pleased to be arriving back in Heraklion, even if it was for just one night.
'Here we are Meli mou. This is the area where I lived when I was a student here.'
Mel took off her helmet and scanned her surroundings.
'No way! That's the pension I worked and lived for a while,' Mel exclaimed as she noted the pension was in disrepair with a few broken windows boarded up.
'I know that pension too. A Greek man and his Dutch wife ran it and then ran away with a substantial amount

of money. I think they scammed the insurance and flooded the roof.'

Mel howled laughing before retelling her story of her friend Rosie and the water tanks on the roof and living in the broom cupboard. It turned out that her and Yannis may have crossed paths as they were in the city at the same time. In fact, Mel's growing suspicion about Yannis' sexuality heightened with the flashback of four years earlier. It had been the day after Rosie had the mishap with the water tanks. Mel had instructed her friend to work on the grapes while Eva's mood had subsided. Mel was late cleaning the only double room in the pension when she knocked on the door. There was no reply so using the master key she let herself in, armed with her mop and bucket.

The sight of two male bodies in the throes of intimacy, one with his toned rear on view with a small tattoo just below a dimple, made her scuttle back out the door. To her relief they checked out a few hours later, never to be seen again. But the tattoo was etched in her memory. She waited for Yannis to confirm that he had in fact stayed at the pension with his male friend but apart from the initial shock on his face, followed by a nervous laugh he gave nothing away. She didn't question him, realising he could have been experimenting and might even be bi sexual.

Although it was approaching winter, the night was kind to them as they met Yannis's friends from university and had a meal in a restaurant overlooking the harbour.

A Lock up on Crete

To Mel's delight, Yannis had booked a room at a nearby hotel instead of staying at one of his friends. After the previous night's alcohol induced sleep, she was grateful of a good shower before sliding into her own single bed, a mere metre away from Yannis. Both friends slept soundly.

The next morning, fresh from a good night sleep, they took the national road to Agios Nikolaos. There was just one more person Yannis wanted to say hello to. Although she had her faults, his Aunt Apollonia was his mama's sister and she had supported his mamma through the nightmare of his brother's brushes with the law. He owed her a visit at least.

The roads were relatively clear as they left the big city and passed the airport on their left. The three lanes soon reduced to two lanes as Yannis drove his motorbike with ease, negotiating the tight bends and tunnels. Mel shivered whenever they passed the roadside memorials of miniature white chapels adorned with photographs of the deceased. They were quite plentiful she thought as they passed signs for Hersonnisos and Malia, the up and coming tourist resorts, so she had heard. The road left the coastline and headed inland. Yannis pointed to their right as a watch tower came into view. She couldn't make out what he was saying but she assumed he was pointing out the imposing prison with the barbed wire fencing. She thought to herself that it was a bizzare siting for a prison, perched on top of the national road, peering down to the town of Neapoli like a bird of prey. At least it was a warning landmark for all those potential

A Lock up on Crete

criminals - if there were many. She made a note to ask about the crime rate in Crete. What this trip had taught her was that she really hadn't seen enough of Crete or delved into its rich history and traditions. There was so much more to Crete than Ierapetra (not that there was anything wrong with the town), but it was her intention to visit more places for sure.

Agios Nikolaos

An hour later they drove slowly into the coastal town of Agios Nikolaos, which undoubtedly was a picture postcard town. It oozed perfection and sophistication and still had a buzz about it in winter. As it was a working town there was a large population of permanent residents. They parked up and immediately sat down at the front of the small fishing harbour.

'What a gorgeous place this town is Yannis,' Mel said as she looked over at the little bridge that separated the harbour from a good sized lake, surrounded by steep limestone rock.

'Yes it is one of my favourite towns too. Do you know the history?' Yannis, once again was eager to enrich his good friend on the myths of Crete. Before Mel had responded to his question, he imparted his information.

'That deep lake you see is Lake Voulesmeni. It is surrounded by myths and legends of course. A local urban myth is that the lake is bottomless and the crater of an extinct volcano connected with the volcanic island crater of Santorini. Also it is reputed that the goddess Athena bathed in it. You know us Greeks like to celebrate,' Yannis explained as Mel nodded her head between sips of Frappe. 'Every Easter, the whole town gathers around the lake with fireworks and firecrackers. It is noisy as you can imagine. I remember when I was a boy and we used to have a special trip to take part. Happy memories Meli mou,' Yannis reflected as he acknowledged a man on a scooter zooming by. It seemed to Mel that from town to town a Cretan person had many connections and cousins, of course. She loved life in Crete with the slower pace and a more general acceptance of all that is good and equally not so good. She also loved spending time with Yannis and although she had now figured he was probably bi sexual and didn't harbour any sexual feeling for her. Although at first she was disappointed she was content with them being good friends. After all, it is usually difficult for a female to have a male friend who doesn't have an ulterior motive! She therefore, counted herself lucky and privileged.

Unfortunately, the upbeat mood changed like the wind as Yannis made his way over to the other side of the harbour. Yannis' aunt Apollonia dumped the laundry on the floor and shrieked like a banshee as she threw her thin arms around him.

'Yanni, Yanni agori mou (my boy)

Both women immediately recognised each other as Mel stepped back in an effort to exit the launderette.

'Yanni, Yanni. What are you doing with that touristee? She is a thief! A dirty thief! She stole from Manolis Mariakis.'

Mel hurried across the harbour to the famous lake. She skimmed its surface, enraged that their perfect trip had

A Lock up on Crete

been spoilt by the interfering old witch. Worse still, not only was she Damianos's aunt but also Yannis's aunt which therefore meant Yannis and Damianos must be cousins. But why hadn't they said? There again who isn't anyone's cousin here in Crete! They were plentiful, after all.

After taking her rage out on the smooth pebbles she had expertly skimmed into the lake, she made her way to the outdoor café with the launderette in view. She could just about make out their outlines as they flung their arms in the air in turn. She knew she wasn't guilty but could not stay for the verbal onslaught from Apollonia. What made it worse was the fact that Apollonia spoke good English and the verbal attack would have been for Mel to understand rather than be shielded from it had it been yelled in Greek. Whatever Yannis made of this altercation, she wasn't sure. All she was sure of was that she was not guilty. In fact while they were here in town, she would go to Manolis Mariakis and explain that she hadn't given him the forgery because she had paid for the bill with a 2000 note not a 10000 one which Tia had handed to her from their pooled purse.

'Let me explain Yanni.' Mel noticed the slight change in his demeanour as he joined her at the café.
'No need to Melissa,'
'Hey what's with the Melissa? You always call me Meli mou – my honey,' Mel suddenly felt her Sunday name had been used in order to reprimand her.

A Lock up on Crete

'Well I have never asked you if I could call you Meli mou and I thought well maybe you prefer your full name.'
Mel felt a pang of anxiety as in the space of half an hour and a visit to the local witch, their relationship had been soured. She chided herself for not staying with them and defending herself. Just what had been said between aunt and nephew, she would probably never find out.
'Pou pas, pou pas? (where are you going),' Yannis called after Mel as she threw some coins onto the table and made her way up a side street.
'To Manolis Mariakis' kafenio!' Mel stomped up the hill, still in earshot of Yannis.
'Don't bother. He is in hospital,' Yannis cried after her.
She carried on regardless, passing Manolis Mariakis' kafenion. There was a sign loosely taped to the window – she assumed the Greek words said it was closed due to illness. She arrived a few minutes later at the bus station and was just in time to step on the bus to Iraepetra. She was glad Yannis had followed her and seen her on the bus. At least he wouldn't wonder where she was. He would drop her small bag off at Medusa's she pre-empted as the bus pulled out of the busy station. She also wondered why Manolis Mariakis had ended up in hospital and exactly what Apollonia had said to Yannis.

Chapter 8

Tia and Andreas, Iraepetra

A Lock up on Crete

Tia and Andreas returned from their idyllic stay in Vai with a promise to Andreas's uncle that they would return when the palm seedlings eventually arrived. Tia had been more than happy that instead of the planting, they had been able to have some much needed privacy together. Wherever they went they were never alone it seemed. Relatives, friends and rivals always seemed to get in the way of any time alone they had. It really was different from back home Tia thought. People back home waited for an invitation to visit each other. Here they just strolled in your home without knocking or any warning – even in the restaurants and bars when it was blatantly obvious you wanted to be alone. People would just plonk themselves down in the middle of them and start jabbering away. It wasn't like the local social club back home that was for sure. She hoped that they would have the chance to return to Vai soon. But for now she had better look for some work again.

<u>Zoe, Iraepetra</u>
Whatever ointment the pharmacy had sold her had worked wonders on the strange blisters in the palms of her hands. Zoe's palms, after a few days application, opened up like a blossoming flower. The pain in in her side had also receded.
Zoe wanted to go back to work the next day but was under strict house rule from Damianos and Katerina not to set a foot out of bed unless to go to the loo. She was surprised to have a visit from Damiano's mother, who only lived next door but since the return from Istanbul hadn't been to see her. She was a heavy set woman with

a few whiskers sprouting from her chin but unlike her sister in law she didn't speak any English. She grunted a few words to Zoe which was translated to '*I am taking over your job.*' Damianos added quickly that it was only temporary until Zoe felt better to return. Zoe smiled but inwardly groaned, hoping that she wouldn't lose her job. After all, his mother, whose name evaded her, might be a dab hand at rubbing cucumbers and the prospect of being allowed out of bed anytime soon was looking rather slim.

That afternoon, Zoe heard a few voices outside her room. It sounded like Katerina but she was curious as to why she was speaking in English. She eased herself from her bed, wrapped the thin dressing gown around her and opened the shuttered windows.
'It is important my patient sleeps and recovers,' she heard Katerina explain to a bemused Tia.
'Katerina , Tia is my friend. Let her in please.' Katerina unfolded her arms and opened the small gate, following Tia to the door of the bedroom.
'Well this is a nice surprise Tia. How are you?' Both friends embraced as Katerina scuttled back to her kitchen. 'Hang on why are you not at work?' Zoe added.
'I quit! Sorry Zoe. You know how I hate getting my hands dirty so Andreas has got me a job at his sister's hair salon. Just washing hair and sweeping up for now but it will probably lead to further when I show them how I can cut hair. Lucky I brought my scissors with me.' Tia enthused as she pulled up a chair at Zoe's bedside.

A Lock up on Crete

'That's great Tia. At least it will be better than rubbing mouldy cucumbers.' Both friends laughed as Zoe continued to tell Tia about Damianos' mother temporarily taking over from her.

'Well if they don't have you back, I'll have a word with Andreas. He seems to be really respected in town and has plenty of contacts.' Tia reassured her friend.

'What line of work is Andreas in then Tia?' Zoe asked leaning back into her heavily embroidered pillow.

'Oh you know, I've not even asked him,' Tia replied, shrugging her shoulders. 'He had to go to Agios Nikolaos to visit one of his sick relatives this morning but he does send you his regards. Anyway, I'd better be off so just get better and follow your nurse's instructions,' Tia winked as Katerina, who must have been listening outside the door, escorted Tia from her property.

'Thanks Tia. By the way did you and Mel see my note about Cara?'

'Yes we did. We're halfway through solving the mystery. But you just rest and we will reveal all when you're better.'

After being administered her medicine from Katerina, Zoe was instructed to sleep. As she lay on the bed, thoughts raced through her mind. What had the girls found out about Cara? Had Cara really stole her identity? She needed to find out. Eventually she succumbed to the effects of the medication and slept until the raised voices of Daminaos and his mother woke her as they returned from work. Damianos and his aunt were in the kitchen as she tried to decipher if they were having a loud chat or they were arguing. It was nigh on impossible to tell with the Greek people unless you were actually looking at them or had a slight idea what they may be discussing. Half an hour passed without even a peep into her bedroom from Damianos to see how she was.

The truth was, she felt as though events were happening too fast and she was losing touch with her friends. Although they still had the apartment, the three of them had their own separate lives going on and were now like passing ships in the night. She wished it was just the three of them again. Maybe they should have kept moving on around the island rather than staying and working in one place.

The next week Katerina discharged her patient declaring she was now fit for work. Zoe could have told her she was fit enough the week previous but had actually enjoyed Katerina's company plus she had already paid her rent in advance for the apartment so she wasn't desperate for cash just yet. Her nursemaid had taught her some valuable Greek phrases and warned her about the offensive phrases she might hear from the younger Greeks. The one she said was worthy of jail. Zoe made a mental note of it then wrote it in her notebook. Of course Katerina had also fed her like a refugee and treated her to traditional Cretan cooking and baking. She reflected on how they had both sat outside in the small yard on stools as they pulled the bright orange flower heads off the aubergine plants and carefully cleaned them to be used for wrapping around rice and meat mixtures – the same as vine leaves are used. Katerina gave Zoe her special Cretan shortbread recipe; the smell of them cooking was just divine and the taste was truly the best she had ever tasted. And dare she say it, even better than the best shortbread she had devoured with endless cups of tea with her mother on a rainy English afternoon. Her heart missed a beat as her thoughts took her back home to the large conservatory at the back of her mother's house. The house she had grown up in. She remembered clearly how her late father had initially not been in favour of the huge glass monstrosity as he called it. Zoe knew full well that her DIY father had other plans for the back garden. She had seen his hand drawn plans for a large shed with a lean too greenhouse.

Zoe returned to the apartment after Katerina insisted she could not possibly walk the ten minutes it would take her. Instead, she sent her off and paid for a taxi. She was greeted at the front door by Theo who had been collecting the rent.
'Ahh kalimera Zoe. I heard from Damianos that you took ill in Istanbul. Pah! Damn those Turks! I hope you feel much better now you are home,' Theo boomed as he helped her with her small bag upstairs to the apartment. 'And one thing please. Zoe, it is dangerous and very expensive to use the electric hob to heat up the apartment. Electricity is very expensive here on Crete. In fact I will bring you more blankets. Take care and see you soon. Oh and I do believe your apartment is up to date with the rent.'
Zoe smiled as she thanked Theo. He was a nice chap overall. Obviously he had to tell them about the rules as he was their landlord but he had kindly eyes and she

noticed how much taller and slimmer he was than most Cretan males.

Once inside she inspected the apartment, desperate to see if she had left her locket here before going to Istanbul. In hindsight, she should really have left it back in the UK but it had always been a source of comfort when she was feeling a little lonely or out of sorts. She desperately missed opening the clasp and seeing the miniscule black and white photos of her mum and dad smiling up at her. She had also searched for it just before leaving her room at Katerina's. She had asked Katerina if she had seen it but received a rather blank response, almost as though she was accusing her of taking it.

After a final but futile attempt of searching every nook and cranny, she gave up and sat on her bed feeling quite down. As she looked around the sparse apartment she noticed that Mel had kept it spic and span and she had placed some wild flowers in a glass jar on Zoe's bedside table. She often wondered if Mel ever felt pressure to look after Zoe and Tia to a certain extent as it had been her idea to come to Iraepetra. Zoe hoped she and Tia weren't too much of a burden to Mel. She also wondered about Yannis and Mel and if they were an item; maybe if the mood was right she might broach the subject - maybe after a few beers. The winter sun crept around the apartment building as Zoe shut the thin curtains and closed her eyes.

She woke up with a start as the apartment door slammed with the wind rushing up the stairwell.

'Who is it?' she shouted as footsteps sounded in the kitchen along with sobbing.

'It's me Mel. Is that you Zoe? I thought nobody was here. Sorry to wake you.'

Mel entered the bedroom with tears streaming down her face.

'Oh my God, what's happened Mel? Is it your family back home?'

'No, no. I'm just being too sensitive that's all. Must be time of month coming up,' she assured Zoe handed her a tissue from the communal box.

Mel relayed the events in Agios Nikolaos with Yannis as Zoe nodded and listened to her friend. Both girls came to the conclusion that to put Mel's mind at rest they should enquire about the welfare of old Manolis Mariakis and if possible when he was out of hospital they should go to Agios Nikolaos and visit him. They needed to establish that they did not pay with a 10,000 drachma note that night. If only they could prove that it was the 2000 drachma note they had paid for their food with. But that seemed quite impossible as it would have been banked. Besides how could they have identified it?

Zoe wondered if this was the right time to change the conversation.

'Mel. Tell me if you don't want to talk but have you and Tia progressed with the matter of Cara's passport?'

'It's ok we can talk about it. Besides it will do me good. Let me just make a brew. Do you want another Zoe?'

'Yes go on then. A good cuppa solves everything as they say back home,' Mel's eyes crinkled slightly at the corners as she rummaged in her work bag for the fresh shortbread she had just lovingly baked.

'Yes, so Tia and I read your note about Cara's passport. We both agreed that it seemed too much of a coincidence that she had used the same name as yours.'

'I totally agree,' Zoe nodded as she allowed her friend to continue.

'Well we did a mind map coming up with all the scenarios. We realised that none of us really knew her surname anyway. Unless you did Zoe?'

'No I didn't and I suppose Cara didn't know mine either.'

'Okay so we got to that point and then thought - why did she use her middle name of Cara rather than her first name, Zoe.' Mel reached in her bedside drawer to retrieve the passport. 'It's hard to see with all this water damage but there isn't any middle name included and I think by law you do have to submit all your names on a passport application. Tia commented that if the name had read - *Zoe Cara Matthews* then she might have preferred to be known as Cara.'

'Hey so what's wrong with Zoe?' Zoe admonished as she licked her lips and devoured her third shortbread.

'Now don't get so defensive Zoe. You never know why and besides, if she was using her middle name Cara, she wouldn't have revealed that her Christian name was the same as yours because she probably didn't like the name!' Mel explained as Zoe lifted her eyes in mock disgust.

'So if all that is true and she is now probably in Italy I wonder how she got through the border without a passport?' Zoe continued.

A Lock up on Crete

'Well we looked in the other clothes she left for any more clues but there were no random documents or anything. Tia came up with the conclusion that she was a bit of a loner with no fixed address as she had mentioned something about being an orphan and her parents had only ever owned a static caravan on a park somewhere in Devon. They apparently moved from Northern Ireland in a hurry when she was younger she told Tia.

'Oh right. Well it's very uncanny and I suppose it is just a coincidence but I can tell you I was a bit freaked out about it when I saw my name under her photo!,'

'I bet you was! Oh, Tia and I have been checking at the poste restante every day to see if there is a letter from Cara but there's nothing yet.'

'You mean Cara or Zoe!'

'Hmmm, that's a thought. Well we will keep checking the poste restante anyway and if she writes to us with a forwarding address we can resume the mystery then. However, no doubt she will be in Italy anyway with a new passport by now.'

'Or a new identity!' Zoe couldn't help feeling there was more to this Cara/Zoe saga but obviously had to accept the logic her friends had concluded. She realised that she may have taken it too far as Mel was clearly still upset with the Yannis and Apollonia dilemma.

Chapter 9

Andreas

A Lock up on Crete

Andreas arrived back in Iraepetra as Tia had just finished her first day at his sister's Maria's salon. He looked perturbed as he walked past the window and continued up the road. 'Andreas, Andreas, ella, ella,' shouted Maria. Andreas continued on his way as both women returned to the clearing away of the mountain of hair on the tiled floor. Tia was relieved when Andreas returned to the salon and took his sister in a hard embrace before turning to Tia and kissing her lightly on her forehead. Sister and brother spoke in rapid Greek.

Andreas directed Tia to a small taverna she had not been in before next to the small port of Ireapetra.
'What's happened, Andreas?'
'My uncle Manolis died this morning.'
'Oh I am so sorry Andreas. Is that why you had to go to Agios Nikolaos?' Tia shuffled closer to him as her hand looped in his.
'Yes. On my last visit I thought he seemed to be not quite himself – a bit vague. He has owned a kafenion there since he was a young man. It's been handed down throughout the generations.'
Suddenly the penny dropped or Tia.
'Oh my Lord, is your uncle Manolis the one that we had the forged note business with?'
'Po,po,po. It must be! Why didn't I realise before?'
Andreas ordered two Metaxa brandies for them from the waiter who had been hovering nearby.
Tia realised that they had come to this particular taverna as it was probable that Andreas wasn't a local here and they could talk in private, out of earshot.

A Lock up on Crete

'Po, po, po! I don't believe it. My poor uncle must have been suffering from some kind of forgetfulness and mistakenly accused you girls. And another thing I don't understand is why Damianos didn't say anything about Apollonia being his aunt!

'That is strange if Damianos knew it was his aunt who accused us in the kafenion Alexis that first morning. Unless he doesn't get on with her maybe? But the christening! Apollonia had been at the christening and Damianos had too.' Tia added, wondering how Apollonia knew the girls would be in Iraepetra. Had Damianos alerted her? He was after all the one who approached Zoe and took us to Theo and the apartment. He seemed to have targeted the three of them from the very start and subtly sorted things out for them – maybe just a little too helpful as she had initially thought. She knew she should give him the benefit of the doubt but would however keep a close eye on Damianos. There was just something about him from the start she couldn't quite put her finger on.

'My uncle did not marry so I am obliged to organise his funeral and make the kafenion secure. Thankfully I do have the code for the safe,' Andreas explained to Tia, who he had fallen head over heels with and knew she could be trusted.

After Andreas had walked Tia home to get an early night in preparation for her second day at Maria's, Andreas caught up with his sister who lived across the road.

'Be careful of Damianos, Andreas. I don't trust him – he is too similar to his aunt Apollonia.

A Lock up on Crete

Maria was two years his junior and had been in the same class at school as Damianos.

The next day Andreas rang his current employer who had given him a hefty amount of irrigation work for him to oversee, informing them that he would be taking a few days off due to family matters. He enjoyed being self-employed as it gave him the opportunity to look after his family when needed. Family was the most important thing in most Cretan's lives. At a drop of a hat, a Cretan was expected to help his immediate and extended family with the olive harvest or similar. It was their duty: any family member not conforming were duly frowned upon and even in some cases, ostracised.

Andreas took the code for the safe from his safe and the spare keys and prepared to drive to Agios Nikolaos. Outside the forlorn looking kafenion, he wondered who had stuck a notice to the closed door. Whoever it was had no right too as he tried to decipher the poor spelling. It was strange as the words were a mixture of Greek and what could be Albanian. Andreas noted that the kafenion already had taken on the appearance of an abandoned building. He turned the brass key in the door and let himself in. Inside, he crossed himself as a faded picture of the Virgin Mary and child looked upon all who entered from the far wall. It would have been hanging there for an eternity; if walls could talk, Andreas mused as he made his way to the counter. Instinctively he washed and dried the crockery and soaked the tarnished brikis, in weak bleach. The brikis were a comfort to him as every home had at least two, used to heat the thick

Greek coffee in. He took out the safe key from his pocket and carefully turned it in its lock. At first the lock wouldn't budge. He wondered if his uncle had changed the safe but realised that it was as old as the kafenion itself. He tried again. A little bit of force and the safe door creaked open. Andreas took a step back as tattered brown envelopes crammed into the safe, sprang free. Each envelope was securely taped up and dated. He was just about to empty the safe when he thought otherwise. He needed a witness, at least for his own piece of mind. He thought about who best to ask and decided he would make the short walk up the hill to the lawyer his uncle may have appointed. Sure enough not five minutes away, the lawyer confirmed that he was indeed his uncle's lawyer and had just received word the day before of his sad passing.

The lawyer took his lunch early and followed Andreas down to the kafenion. They counted forty envelopes stuffed into the safe. Exhaling, Andreas selected one from the back and one from the front. The envelopes were dated back from a year previous to the week before Manolis Mariakis had the massive stroke that had ended his life.

Carefully and with the lawyer as his witness, he opened each one. The envelopes contained one week's takings in cash along with the receipts. He had to hand it to his late uncle- he had been spot on with his accounts. But why had he not banked for over a year? The lawyer advised Andreas to wait until the next day where he would set aside a few hours and count the envelopes with him and make a legal entry of the total amount.

A Lock up on Crete

That night Andreas stayed in a modest hotel rather than the back room of the kafenion where his uncle had lived most of the time. The late shifts plus the copious amount of alcohol he would consume with his friends resulted in him rolling on to his roll- away bed until the cockerel in the back yard would wake him up for another day at his kafenion. He had been a proud man and had run it all by himself without the need of help. The only help he would have considered was Apollonia but she always seemed to be busy in the launderette, the pension/guest rooms or running up and down the hill to and from the bus station. Manolis and Apollonia really should have been man and wife with children to take over his business but it wasn't to be. Maybe a few snatched hours when she had the time and was in the mood was all it amounted to. Manolis could never quite let it go, why she hadn't jumped at the chance to marry an owner of a kafenion plus the enviable owner of a traditional cottage overlooking the most enviable view for miles around. Basically it had baffled him all his life and what he did give her on her visits to him clearly hadn't been enough!

Andreas had his evening meal around the lake, sheltering from the cool breeze inside the restaurant. The customers were sparse which allowed the owner to join him with a small bottle of Raki as they reminisced about Old Manolis Marinakis. He felt better having spoken with people and feeding his stomach with nutritious food. He walked back up the street to his

A Lock up on Crete

guest house and hoped it wasn't too late to phone Tia. After the third ring he was about to hang up in fear of waking her when she answered.

'Hello,'

'Hello Tia agape mou. I hope I didn't wake you. I have been to the kafenion and now I am at the small hotel ready for sleep. Did your second day go ok?' Andreas coiled the telephone wire around his finger as he imagined her with her hairnet on.

'Andreas, I'm glad you rang. Your sister wasn't sure if you knew which lawyer your uncle appointed and she had just remembered which one it was,' Tia whispered, not wanting to wake Zoe and Mel as she stood in the hallway at the phone point.

Andreas quickly filled Tia in about the safe and the stash of envelopes.

'Andreas, I have remembered something that you might be able to help me with. Since the witch Apollonia accused Mel of giving Manolis that forged note, well it dawned on me today when I went to the bank,' Tia babbled.

'You have lost me Tia. What is this 'dawning on me' I'm not sure of this phrase.'

'Sorry. I mean I remembered something about the accusation. When I was on my lunch break I went to the bank for Maria to pay her bill and the cashier handed me a 2000 drachma note with a bit of scribbled writing on. I didn't think anything of it at the time but then during the course of the day I remembered that when we first arrived at Heraklion airport I went to change my pound notes to drachmas and at the time, although I was

A Lock up on Crete

sleepy, I thought it quite strange that one of the notes was old and defaced with scribbled writing in pen on it. Anyway, the three of us had agreed for ease, that I would hold onto our pooled money. At the kafenion, I gave the 2000 drachma note to Mel to pay the bill. So Andreas, what I am saying is that when you open the envelope tomorrow for that week's takings, look to see if the 2000 drachma note with the writing on it is there. It looked like someone had added up with a simple sum on the note. If it is in the envelope then that will definitely, once and for all, prove that we are innocent and that Apollonia has made the whole accusation up!'

'Tia, I will, but I will wait until the lawyer joins me and I will tell him what you have told me. I will call you at the salon straight away. Now try to get some sleep and I will see you tomorrow evening agape mou.'

'Kala nichta, agape mou,' Tia replied as she willed herself to get to sleep. After all, she needed her energy for the salon. She hadn't said anything to Andreas but his sister kept nipping out most of the day leaving Tia to explain to the clients in very broken Greek that she would be back soon. It was getting a bit embarrassing. However, she felt she had made a good impression and settled in well.

Very early the next morning Andreas phoned the lawyer to ask if he could come to the kafenion earlier than planned. Andreas was exhausted and had hardly slept, hoping that what Tia had told him would be proven. He didn't like confrontations generally and had always been the peace maker and the level headed male about town. However, he remembered from his childhood that

A Lock up on Crete

Apollonia, both Damianos and Yannis's aunt, had caused
enough trouble in Iraepetra during her lifetime.
Although she was never proven of any wrongdoing, it
was her malicious gossip that had split up lovers, families
and friends. The whole town had rejoiced when she left
for Agios Nikolaos some years ago. Then, like a bad wart
she had shown up at Alexis' kafenion trying to accuse
Mel of the forged note. He still couldn't fathom out why
his uncle had so smitten with her – enough for him to
never marry.
Fortunately, the police had dealt with her on numerous
occasions and with this in mind the older policeman that
had served at the station for many years had been
lenient with the girls.

The 2000 drachma note with the scribbled sum sprawled
over it was sealed in a plastic bag to be sent to the police
station for evidence. The lawyer had signed it along with
Andreas and had taken charge of the whole affair.
Andreas couldn't wait to call Tia with the good news but
had to wait confirmation that Mel's fingerprints which
were held at the police station in Iraepetra, were also on
the note. He knew himself that the note would have
multiple fingerprints but also knew that it was just a
formality and as it wasn't a serious accusation as such, it
would soon be dealt with and closed. He knew too that
the police had more important cases to deal with. Thus,
it would be up to the people of Iraepetra to spread the
word about the outcome and any suspicion that anyone
had about the girls would be cleared.

A Lock up on Crete

Andreas wanted to treat the lawyer to lunch so they walked the short distance to a relatively new trendy café bar overlooking Lake Voulismeni from the top of the small cliff. He liked the young lawyer as they spoke about their respective school days and families. The lawyer was originally from Thessaloniki but had been tempted when a colleague had asked him to start up a partnership in Crete. The young lawyer soon realised he had made the right choice as he embraced the slower pace of life, the cuisine and the filoxenia. The demand for their conveyancing was plentiful. He explained that Crete had seen a surge in overseas property development and construction. Malia and Hersonnisos were fast becoming rivals to the likes of Ayia Napa in Cyprus and Falaraki in Rhodes as hedonistic party resorts. Andreas wasn't so keen on the information as he didn't want his beloved Crete to open up its doors to drunken behaviour and drugs like he had heard about on the other islands. After a pleasant lunch, the two men shook hands and parted company.

Back at the kafenion, Andreas began to dial his sister's salon when he was beaten to it by the incoming call from Tia.
'Yes Tia, I know I should have phoned earlier but I am waiting for the police to call with the results of the fingerprints,'
'You mean you found the 2000 note Andreas?' Tia whispered into the phone trying to supress her excitement.

A Lock up on Crete

'Yes, yes we did and it is now at the police station so I will call you when we have news but I think I will take a walk there myself and clear my head.' His headache had started that morning and wasn't intent on subsiding as he shut up the kafenion and walked the few streets, passing the large hospital and down to the police station.

Once inside, he was ushered into a smaller office where a large policeman handed him over the 2000 note. It had been impossible to decipher all the fingerprints on them. The policeman congratulated Andreas as having the foresight to appoint the lawyer as a witness. In his eyes that was enough evidence to prove the girls were not guilty - especially as the note wasn't even a forgery! Andreas thanked the policeman for the results from the fingerprint test, knowing full well no one would have had the time or enthusiasm to liaise with the police in Iraepetra where Mel's fingerprints were kept. It was a matter of appeasement and the less police time wasted the better.

He relayed the results to Tia as soon as he returned to the kafenion.

'I know it puts us in the clear, but what now?' she asked.

'I will keep the note in the safe and if Apollonia or anyone else mentions the note in the future we have the evidence at our fingertips. He heard Tia titter in the background at his faux pas. 'Tia, I think that most people know what she is capable of anyway and will not think badly of you three girls. So please don't worry agape mou but you can now tell Mel and Zoe that the case has been solved and unfortunately my uncle was either

A Lock up on Crete

suffering more from dementia than anyone knew or Apollonia was up to her tricks again. Whatever it was, one thing is clear and the three of you will not lose any respect in Iraepetra from now on.'

'I'm so relieved Andreas. When are you coming back to Iraepetra?'

'Tomorrow hopefully. I just need to complete some more paperwork here and then I will be
back to take care of the funeral arrangements.'

'Are you taking care of everything yourself Andreas? Will your sisters help at all?'

'No it is the eldest son's work - but it is good. I am looking forward to seeing you Tia.'

No sooner had Tia placed the phone on the receiver, Maria wanted the conversation relaying to her. As there were only two older women in the salon and they were under the hairdryers, Tia relayed the news about the update of the banknote.

After the last two clients had paid she bid Maria goodnight, thankful she didn't have to be in the salon until noon the next day.

It had taken just a few hours for news to spread all over Iraepetra about the solving of the banknote. Unbeknown to Maria and Tia, the last two women in the salon the previous day, had between them, pieced together enough of Tia and Maria's hushed conversation to decipher its content. Plus, the two clients were ex English tutors and although they had only told one person each that evening, by the next morning, at least two thirds of Iraepetra were now caught up to speed

A Lock up on Crete

about the three touristees and Apollonia's accusation. It really wasn't too much of a surprise!

Chapter 10

Mel

Mel returned to work where she felt she could hold her head up high. Even though no one had mentioned the banknote fiasco and no one had treated her any differently, she just had that feeling that there had been a minority of accusing eyes around town, particularly at work when on a few occasions her boss struggled to sell any of her baking and would have to feed it to the opportunist cats that patrolled the skip at the back of the kitchens. Now, the only thing that made her feel sad was the hasty departure of Yannis in Agios Nikolaos. She assumed that he had returned his motorbike to his parents' home and left for Cyprus earlier than planned. If only they hadn't gone to visit his aunt Apollonia. Damn that woman! If he had mentioned her name beforehand, Mel would have been able to explain all to Yannis. And now he had gone and she missed him as a dear friend. Apollonia had an awful lot to answer for that was for sure!

It was lunchtime and the morning had flown as Mel had turned out a record number of apple tarts, bakewell tarts and bread and butter puddings. It had felt good to weigh out her ingredients and sift the flour. She had always felt baking cathartic, kneading her worries away

A Lock up on Crete

and stirring her thoughts in a mixing bowl. As usual, she went out for some fresh air and walked the whole length of the seafront before taking up her usual place in her local taverna and perusing the menu.

'I hear that you are the one baking at Medusa's,' a waitress she didn't recognise commented as she hovered to take her order.

'Yes I am.' Mel replied with a courteous smile. 'And why do you ask?' she added.

'I hear that they sell well that is all. Now what would you like to order?'

Mel had lost her appetite as she flicked the lettuce around on her Greek salad wondering why there was lettuce there in the first place. A traditional Greek salad –horiatiki, is never served with lettuce. If you wanted lettuce, then that was a separate dish altogether. She paid her bill and left. It was only when she looked at the sign of the taverna that she realised she had been in the wrong taverna and sheepishly hurried by her usual. She chuckled to herself, realising that she must obviously be more upset than she realised about Yannis. She would ask Zoe that evening to ask Damianos if he had spoken to his cousin before he left for Cyprus.

Zoe

Zoe returned to the cucumber factory along with Damianos and his mother. His mother, whose name still evaded Zoe had been made permanent – obviously a dab hand with the cucumbers! From the very moment they piled into the pickup truck that next morning, Zoe felt less welcome than she had before. Without Tia being

A Lock up on Crete

by her side she felt the dynamics had changed. She counted even more Greek women than before crammed into the small space who all gave her the evil eye when she climbed in. Suddenly, as the pickup pulled onto the main road, the younger women banged on the cab door. The pick -up screeched to a halt. Like an animal stampede, the women piled out of the truck, gathered their long skirts and ran over the road to the olive groves. Like wild animals each woman furiously ripped green foliage from the earth, returning with the deep green leaves stuffed into their aprons.

'Horta, horta,' the oldest one explained to Zoe pursing her lips in a kiss. Zoe smiled and nodded. Whatever it was it looked like giant dandelion leaves to her but there again what she had been taught at Katerina's was that the Cretan's made full use of their land and its produce. Maybe it was a weed that they ate. She would ask Damianos, who was currently riding in the passenger seat in the cab engaged in animated conversation with Costas.

It had been like starting a new job as Zoe took her place before the cucumber vat. Most of the tourist workers had moved on and there were more Yiayia's than before she had left for Istanbul. Zoe feared for her job as she felt more alone than ever. Damianos' mother didn't help either by constantly chunnering away to her friends then glaring over at Zoe. By the way she pointed to her hands and side she was inevitably telling them all about the virus she had picked up in Istanbul; she could imagine her warning them not to come too close to her. Then

A Lock up on Crete

again, despite her harsh looks, she could have been equally saying how worried she had been for her. If only she knew more Greek!

Damianos had also made his presence known as he bossed the two Egyptian boys about on the upper line of the machinery. Zoe chuckled to herself as she spotted them giving Damianos the V sign behind his back.

At the end of the day it was just another day in the cucumber factory and Zoe was glad to be back earning again.

Chapter 11

The funeral of Manolis Mariakis, Agios Nikolaos

'In Greek culture we believe the soul does not leave the body until three days after the person has died. The family will visit the grave for the three days after burial to look after the soul. We can ask the priest to conduct a small ceremony where he will bless a plate of koliva and scatter it into the wind. Then he will break the plate onto the tombstone.' Andreas explained the tradition of the funeral to Tia in preparation as they shared a small meal that evening on his return from Agios Nikolaos.

Tia was intrigued and wanted to be more than prepared for the special funeral.

'What is the koliva dish Andreas?'

'Koliva is made of wheat berries that represent the promise of everlasting life, raisins which symbolise the

A Lock up on Crete

sweetness of life and spices which are symbols of plenty.'

'Oh please tell me more Andreas and then I will know what the funeral will be like for you. Maria has asked me to look after her salon as she has a few booked in already and knows that I can cut hair but the yiayias only want a shampoo and set so I can do that on my own,'

'No Tia. You will be at my side for the funeral. I am also inviting Zoe and Mel if they can attend.'

'What? Surely it is for family and well you know, us three being the touristees and all that.' Tia wondered how other family and friends would react to three touristees attending the funeral, whom until recently, had been suspects in the bank note fiasco.

'Tia this is my say in all matters to do with my uncle's funeral. It will resolve all the previous bad feelings. It is what I want and I am sure it is what my uncle would have wanted if he had known the truth. So Tia, I will tell Maria she will have to shut the salon.'

Tia knew Andreas wouldn't take no for an answer as she kissed him tenderly on his lips and wrapped her arm in his. They walked the short distance to her apartment where he said goodnight to her at the front door and asked her to invite Zoe and Mel to the funeral on his behalf.

By the time Tia had arrived at the salon the following lunchtime, Maria already knew that Tia was attending the funeral and thus would have to close the salon for the day. She also recommended that Tia stay with Andreas for three days after the funeral to stay with her uncle's soul until it departed to a better life. Maria knew that she couldn't afford to close the salon for three days, her two other sisters had young children and her parents were too old now so it seemed viable for Tia to stay by Andreas's side. Despite the circumstances, Tia was more than happy to be of service to the family and hoped she was giving off the right emotions.

As she swept the floor of the morning's hair trimmings, Tia picked up the colour chart and made a note of the colour that was closest to her hair colour and then pondered whether to add a streak of dark red.

The salon closed at 4pm as Tia made a special effort to give the floors and surfaces a good scrub and asked Maria about the hair colour.

'Ahh Tia mou, of course you can use the colour. Would you like me to touch up those roots at the back you cannot reach? We can do it now if you like?' Maria smiled at her new staff member having high hopes for her. She knew she cut hair too but needed to take it step by step as she didn't know if she could afford to pay her a stylist wage. Tia smiled back at her employer; she still found it quite hard to accept the kindness of the Cretans or the 'Filoxenia' which translated to 'kindness to strangers.'

A few days later, Tia packed a small suitcase that Cara had left when she went in search of the man from Milan. Tia had dressed in all black after buying a warm black fluffy jacket at a bargain price from the otherwise most expensive clothes shop in Ireapetra. At least she would be able to wear it again as the chilly evening nights crept in. She thought it endearing that, although it was

A Lock up on Crete

winter, there were still plenty of couples, families and friends that enjoyed the frequent warm evenings and would dine 'al freso' in the seafront bars and restaurants.

She walked the short distance to where Andreas' family lived. Andreas was already in Agios Nikolaos. He had performed the duty of watching over the corpse in the humble, but enviably located cottage that his uncle had owned.

'Ahhh Tia mou, Tia mou,' Maria greeted as she introduced her to her elderly parents and her younger sister. Any nerves Tia had envisaged had disappeared as they prepared for the forty minute car journey to Agios Nikolaos and to the funeral of Manolis Mariakis.

There were both similarities and differences to a Greek funeral and a British funeral as Tia took her seat next to Andreas and Maria in the small chapel facing the beautiful Mirabello Bay. At first she winced as mourners took their turn around the open casket to pay their last respects to Manolis , the late, highly respected kafenion owner and lay flowers and items of importance at his side. Andreas's other sister Eleni's little daughter went forward on her own to the casket. Before placing a kiss on her great uncle's forehead, she proudly displayed a small arrangement of dried flowers above her head to the mourners.

Finally and with a silent sigh of relief from Tia, who had struggled to supress her tears, the priest closed the casket and the mourners filed out from the front. Unlike the other Greek celebrations, the funeral procession was

A Lock up on Crete

a quiet affair with less people in attendance than Tia imagined.

Andreas, Tia and Maria, followed by Andreas's parents followed the casket out into the winter sunshine as raised voices could be heard from the back of the chapel.

'My God! Apollonia is here, where she is not welcome,' Andreas seethed through gritted teeth as Apollonia was escorted out of a side door. Tia linked him and squeezed his arm lightly to show she understood. Hopefully, that would be the last they saw of her, Tia hoped. The chapel had been chosen to the close proximity of the burial ground so as to aid the older mourners with the traditional procession on foot.

Once at the burial ground, Tia was amazed to see the large ornate graves meticulously cared for. There were many people already at the graveyard attending family graves as they fell silent and bowed their heads. Eleni's adorable daughter took the flowers from the mourners and laid them all around the final resting place of her great uncle. Maria had explained to Tia a few more of the Greek funeral traditions, this one, the laying of flowers in order to purify the ground around the grave. After the priest had blessed the grave and departed, Tia was taken aback as she saw a van pull up and two men dressed all in black carry the Makaria. Although Maria had mentioned the Makaria was known as the 'meal of blessings' or 'mercy meal, she had not expected it to happen at the graveside. It took her a few minutes to compose herself and take her place at the trestle table which the men had quickly set up with accompanying fold up chairs.

Tia felt she was in some kind of ethereal movie as she soaked in the atmosphere. It was a unique mix of sobriety and enlightenment.

Andreas, catching Tia's expression of wonderment mixed with confusion, explained more.

'It must be different for you Tia. And I am sorry I couldn't prepare you more for our traditions. You see, we didn't have the space in my uncle's home for the 'makaria' as all mourners must attend, so we decide to hold it the more traditional way here at the grave. I'm relieved we have good weather though.' Andreas crossed himself as he looked up to the blue sky.

'It's lovely, Andreas. I'm just overwhelmed by it all to be honest. It's just so different to back home but lovely all the same. Tell me more about the meal please.' Tia pulled her chair closer to Andreas.

'Lipone - so. The Makaria is a celebration of my uncle's life and it is traditional to eat fish. Fish is a sign of fasting and mourning that the deceased has departed this life. We will be mourning for forty days but of course you don't need to, but the whole family will wear black and not participate in any celebrations for this period. I hope you don't find it too distressing Tia as I know in England it is not required.'

Tia squeezed his arm again not quite knowing how to respond. She was surprisingly lost for words today but just wanted to do the right thing for Andreas and his family.

A Lock up on Crete

The Makaria was eventually laid out on the long table and after a toast from Andreas the mourners tucked into an array of dishes from local fish, string beans in tomato sauce, rice pilaf, paximadia (biscotti biscuits) and koulourakia (sweet vanilla bread buns).

Andreas served the cognac and red wine to all who could partake as Maria followed with the pots of coffee. Eleni's daughter placed a carnation into the palm of each mourner.

Suddenly a commotion was heard from across the road. In Greek, Apollonia declared:

'I was his lover. We planned to get married. I am a mourner!'

Again she was escorted swiftly away as the mourners continued with the Makaria, shaking their heads and crossing their hearts.

Andreas, obviously aware that Tia was struggling to comprehend everything, diverted her thoughts by explaining more about the Makaria.

'Take no notice, agape mou. I'm sure we won't see her again. She just had to try and spoil it. However, if you look around you can see that nobody is bothered. Let me tell you more about the Makaria. The name is from Greek mythology of course. Makaria was a goddess and the daughter of Hades who is the god of the underworld. Hades is the one who will look after my uncle's soul.'

'Thank you Andreas. I love hearing about all the myths and traditions. I just hope Apollonia is dragged down to the bottom of the ocean by Aphrodite himself!'

Superficial creases lit up Andreas's eyes as he explained

to Tia that it was the God Hades who was the ruler of the Underworld.

'Agape mou. I think now you can relax knowing that everyone knows how spiteful Apollonia is after the trouble she caused you and your friends. Everyone, including my family know you are all innocent.' Andreas reassured her as Eleni's daughter stood up to sing a short song.

'That child is amazing,' whispered Tia.

'Yes of course. She is my niece,' Tia felt Andreas's strong arms around the small of her back as her body relaxed for the first time in many weeks.

Tia had never spent so much time beside a grave as she did the following three days after the funeral. Everything amazed her about the Greek and Cretan culture and this was no exception. In all honesty she couldn't imagine any family back home having the commitment and time to stay near the deceased's grave to be there when their soul departed the earth to the ethereal; she found it simply endearing. The three days passed quicker than she wanted. They stayed at Manolis's beach cottage and although extremely basic and rustic both inside and outside, the view over Mirabello Bay took her breath away each time she opened the window in the morning. There was also a modest size balcony that led the eye out from the one room to the undeniably jaw dropping vista of the bay. Tia had never witnessed before just how 'blue' the sea and sky were in Greece. Even postcards in the souvenir shops didn't do the real thing justice. There was also another rather incongruously balcony built at the side of the cottage where bougainvillea wound itself in and out of the frame leading into the colourful shrubbery.

By the third day, Andreas had sorted most of the administration of his uncle's business. The hearing of the will was planned for the week after and Tia was already hoping he wanted her by his side again. When she thought back to her life back home and the soured relationship with Chris, it was hard to believe this was now her life and family. She was hoping that the bubble wouldn't burst and now she had completed her trial at the salon she could now demonstrate her true hairdressing talent and commitment.

As the forty day mourning began, she realised that she needed to allow Andreas his space so returned to the apartment. She was also to be able to spend quality time with   Zoe and Mel; they had a lot to catch up with.

Andreas

Andreas had lied a little to Tia. He had told her to return to Iraepetra the next day after the three day vigil and that he would follow a few days later as he still had some odd and ends to finalise with the lawyer. Tia didn't seem to mind as she was intent on returning to the salon to help Maria and show her commitment.

As soon as Andreas had waved goodbye to Tia from the bus station, he immediately paid a visit to the launderette, overlooking the picturesque harbour.

'Stay away from my family Apollonia. You have no right to anything. If you try to engage in any conversation or spread false gossip about the three girls or anyone I

A Lock up on Crete

know, I will have you arrested.' His warning words had flowed like a well-rehearsed speech. He turned to leave as Apollonia treated him to her backlash of hatred that had built up between the two families for many years. 'Your family owe me! You know the truth Andreas or if you don't then care to ask your papa. I expect your mama has no idea about his infidelity,' Apollonia drew breath for a few seconds then continued. 'I will contest the will. Manolis Mariakis and I were engaged to be married and I am classed as his common law wife so the kafenion will be mine and the cottage. You and your family will soon find out. Don't think otherwise.' Andreas didn't reply. He wanted to check that her revelation was true. Had his uncle and Apollonia really been a couple? There had been no evidence of her living in the cottage unless he had missed something that might indicate otherwise. He decided to go straight to his lawyer. And then what had she said about his own papa? Infidelity! Andreas felt his mouth sour as her venom soured around in his head.

'Andreas my friend, I cannot comment as I do not know what the Will will actually say. However, I will find out about the implications on the ruling of a common law wife. Try not to worry Andreas. In fact I have heard of this woman who runs the launderette from a few clients of mine. Of course I cannot divulge any information but I will try my upmost to solve this problem for you and your family.

A Lock up on Crete

Andreas tried to eat that evening in the small taverna up the road which had now taken on the winter business from his late uncle's kafenion. He spoke briefly to Tia who could sense something was bothering him. How close they had become so soon he thought. It felt as though Tia had always been at his side, comforting him and sharing jokes with her wicked sense of humour. If anything surprising did transpire from the will and his uncle had left everything to Apollonia, (why his uncle was so obsessed with her still confounded him), he would obviously be disappointed but he was more than content with his life and new love, Tia.

Andreas was thankful his uncle had appointed such an amenable lawyer as he sat in the comfortable leather sofa in his office the next afternoon.
'Ok Andreas, I have looked into the common law wife issue and unless this woman is stuck in the past, as in Ancient Greece, and unless she can prove that Manolis agreed to marry her on paper, she cannot prove anything unless there is evidence that she had lived with him. Just to clarify, I read in one of my encyclopaedias that in ancient Greece and Rome, marriages were private agreements between individuals and families. Community recognition of a marriage was largely what qualified as a marriage. Religious officials took no part in marriage ceremonies and did not keep registers. It was relatively common for couples to cohabit with no ceremony; cohabiting for a moderate period of time was sufficient to make it a marriage and carried no social stigma.' The lawyer pulled the encyclopaedia down from

A Lock up on Crete

the shelf and turned it round for Andreas to confirm the words with his own eyes.

'If we were in Ancient times then she would have taken everything. Thank the Lord that we are now in these more understanding times,' the lawyer added. Andreas stroked his chin that had a few days growth.

'There is nothing at all in the cottage that looks like it belongs to a woman. It is exceptionally bare, in fact I think my uncle lived most of the time in the kafenion,' Andreas replied with a sigh of relief. The last thing he needed was any complications. He was becoming exhausted from the responsibility of it all and would be relieved when it was all over. That night he slept soundly.

Before he left for Iraepetra, Andreas needed to go to the kafenion to deposit some small trinkets he had found in his uncle's cottage. Although they didn't look valuable, they were still better off in the safe. Locking up the little cottage with a view most people would pay handsomely for, Andreas made the short walk to the kafenion. Reaching into his pocket for the key, he noticed a few marks near to the edge of the door. It looked as though someone had been hacking near the lock with a sharp implement. He knew it hadn't been there before as the day after his uncle had died he had specifically had the locks on both properties professionally changed.

Inside, he placed the trinkets into the safe. It was an exceptional windy day as he listened to it whistle around the building and force its way down the chimney where there was a log burner. Something else caught his

attention too. As he checked the back door, Andreas noticed the curtain flapping and the sash window slightly open. He was sure he had secured everything: he was a meticulous person. He must be tired he thought, as he secured the window again, realising that he must have left it open a crack as the kafenion had become stuffy with the lack of fresh air. Before leaving, he decided to use the phone to call Tia and inform her he was on his way back to Ireapetra. He hoped she had coped in the salon as Maria had asked her to keep shop as she needed to attend the doctors with their mama. Tia didn't pick up which slightly worried him but in hindsight Maria might have told her not to as she wouldn't be able to reply in Greek and most of the older ladies in town hadn't had the education his generation had had the privilege of. With reluctance, he placed the receiver on the hook. As Andreas was a meticulous person, he noticed that the note pad he had brought with him a few days beforehand had been moved from the right hand side of the telephone to the left. He picked it up to replace it to the right as a note fluttered to the floor. It read: *Dear Apollonia I am happy that you have agreed to marry me. We will marry soon and you will be my wife as you have been for many years living with me and looking after me.*
All my Love
 Manolis Mariakis

Andreas's hands shook as an imaginary bullet seared through his chest. He couldn't believe what he was reading. He also knew that it must have been put there

A Lock up on Crete

on purpose and recently by Apollonia. He knew that she had never lived at the cottage that was for sure and probably didn't spend any time in the kafenion either. Unless his uncle stayed with her in the tiny flat above the launderette? He remembered her words at the funeral. She would probably have had a key to the kafenion and as the locks had changed, forced her way into the back and left the note there. But why did she leave it for him to find knowing full well that he could easily discard of it? Maybe she had a duplicate. Wondering what on earth to do for the best, he called Tia again. Still she didn't pick up. There was only one thing for it and that was to dispose of it. He just hoped and prayed that she hadn't coerced Manolis in the days where he wasn't quite with it to agree to marry her and make him write it down. He told himself not to tell a soul about destroying the note. As he made his way to the bus station, Andreas mulled over why on earth his uncle would have been enticed into Apollonia's web in the first place. He also wondered whether he should have kept the note and shown it to the lawyer.

Chapter 12

Zoe, Ireapetra

Zoe had endured the absolute day from hell. Somehow, Damianos's alter ego had kicked in as he strode around the factory floor as if he owned shares in it. The only positive of the day was that he had moved Zoe from the cucumber vat and the gaggle of Greek grannies to the upper machine where the cucumbers were sealed in their protective plastic. At least she didn't have to endure the constant stares and gibes from them. They had been so kind at first to herself and Tia but then it seemed, ever since Damianos's mama had stood in for her during her recuperation, they had changed their attitude towards her. Most of the day, she was on her own at the top end of the conveyer belt; probably why Damianos had moved her there. He epitomised the nastier side of the Greek male – jealousy and possessiveness.

The majority of the cucumbers were exported to Germany. There must have been a huge demand for them as they struggled to complete the orders. Fortunately, for all their sakes there was a unanimous decision in favour of working overtime. During a quick lunch break, Damianos surprised Zoe by asking her if she would like to move into his room at his home with him. She had declined his offer and explained that she had come to Crete to be with her friends but also thanked him for asking. She expected his mama would expect board from her anyway and now, as she had to work with him, she was now even more thankful of her own space at the apartment. Plus, after seeing his alter ego at work, she was thoroughly fed up and contemplated asking Mel if there was any work at the Medusa restaurant.

Mel, Medusa restaurant, Ireapetra

A Lock up on Crete

Mel felt fortunate that she enjoyed her work at Medusa's and so was sad to hear that Zoe's job at the factory wasn't going well; especially now Tia was working in the salon. She worried a little about her friend. Since her trip to Istanbul and her subsequent illness she didn't seem as happy and carefree. Whenever she saw her now at the apartment she was either too tired to chat or seemed pre-occupied with her travel journal she kept with her passport. Mel decided to arrange for a girlie day together. They could hire some scooters and ride along the coast where Yannis had taken her and have some quality time together. Failing that, they could take the bus to Agios Nikolaos and have a leisurely lunch around the lake and a walk along the beach front. She thought the latter would be a better option then they could have a few carafes of wine as long as they made it back to the bus station for the last bus back to Iraepetra. Yes, she would broach the subject later when Tia returned from Andreas's. Tia spent most of her evenings there and it would do them all good to get back to their trio.

Unfortunately, Tia arrived back at the apartment too late to suggest they get together on Sunday and Zoe had fallen asleep reading her book. So, on her way to work, Mel crossed the road to Maria's salon. Tia was already at the salon, busy with her first client of the day. It was surprising to see a male sat in one of the chairs but Tia had suggested to Maria that they have an option for unisex as they did back home. She also had her mother post her barbering certificate to her. Maria was

A Lock up on Crete

overjoyed to welcome their first ever male as Tia specialised in the barbering.

'Tia. Just a quick one – can you join me for lunch today?'

'I'll ask Maria, hold on she's just in the back mixing some colour.' Tia pulled the curtain aside and entered the back of the salon. Mel glanced round at the hairdressing chairs all shiny and black and the shy young male waiting for Tia. He acknowledged Mel with a tight smile as though he didn't know what he was letting himself in for. She wondered if she could hack it talking to customers all day making small talk, but then again how did Tia communicate with them? She would ask her sometime. Mel knew where she belonged and that was in the kitchen, preferably alone with her baking.

'Maria said 2pm. So I'll meet you at Medusa's. Shall we keep it simple and go to your local taverna then?

'Yes. Good idea Tia. See you then,' Mel confirmed as she watched her friend take her scissors out of the jar, tucked an apron around the neck of her first male client and snipped away. Mel had visions of a female version of Edward Scissorhands but obviously would never impart her thoughts to her friend – she just hoped that the young guinea pig wouldn't miss his locks of dark curls too much!

'Is Mr M always so affectionate with you Mel?' Tia asked as they ordered a small carafe of the house white.

'I've not noticed,' Mel replied as she poured them both half a glass of wine.

'Like cuddling you a little longer than necessary with his eyes glued to your chest!' Tia retorted, knowing full well her friend knew what she was getting at.

'Oh you know these Greeks. They don't do subtle. Besides, he said one of the reasons he wanted me back was because he was mesmerised how my chest moves in unison with my cake mixer.' Both girls laughed loudly, catching the attention of a few diners.

'Oh sorry to interrupt you ladies but are you the English baker at Medusa's?' a middle aged man with greying hair and a thick Yorkshire accent asked from the table opposite.

'Yes that's me. Have you bought any of my tarts?' Mel added, feeling quite giddy with her second glass of wine.

'No but my mate has. He says they are spot on and apparently all the ex -pats living in Agios Nikolaos and Elounda have said so too. They get them delivered every week.'

Mel blushed and told him to go to Medusas in an hour if he was still in town and she would give him a free sample.

'My name's Bill,' he said as he held out his hand.

'I'm Mel and this is my friend Tia.'

Bill took Mel's hand and shook it hard before paying his bill and giving the girls a little salute as he left the taverna.

'Ahhh, cute but definitely too old.'

'Too old for you Tia?' Mel asked stroking her hand where Bill had touched it.

A Lock up on Crete

'No silly. I'm not interested. I mean you of course, unless you like the older silver foxes?' Tia teased as they tucked into their moussaka. Mel paused for a moment.

'Tia. I am quite worried about Zoe.'

'You read my mind Mel! Me too,' Tia replied as she arranged her cutlery on the table and waited in anticipation for her lunch.

Chapter 13

Sunday, Elounda – 4 miles from Agios Nikolaos

Tia, Zoe and Mel arrived at the bus station in Agios Nikolaos before taking the next bus to Elounda, just four miles down the coast. Tia had mentioned that Elounda was reportedly to have one of the best fish tavernas in the whole of East Crete and it was idyllically situated on a floating pontoon with the beautiful Mirabello bay as a backdrop.

Mel checked the time for the return bus on the faded timetable stuck to the lamppost. Before finding the restaurant, they had a stroll along the deserted beach before heading back towards the few restaurants that were still open. The bells from the village church chimed as families piled out before descending on the tavernas for a catch up and a coffee. The girls soaked up the winter sun as they stopped to take a few photos of each other with the backdrop of the bright blue and yellow small fishing boats tied up in the square shaped harbour.

'Isn't it just so quaint and calm?' Tia said as they approached the floating restaurant recommended by one of the Yiayias she'd given a shampoo and set to a few days earlier.

'It really is. Everything is so vivid in the sunshine. I suppose when it's cloudy it doesn't look so good though,' Zoe added as they were shown to their seats at the front of the pontoon.

'Zoe, why all the doom and gloom just lately?' Mel enquired as she handed her a menu.

'Oh I wasn't aware of I was being like that. I just mean well you know back home when the sun comes out, even the drabbest of places look good. It's just a comparison. Am I really coming across like that?' Tia took a deep breath and took over from Mel who nodded her agreement.

'Zoe. Mel and I have noticed lately and since returning from Istanbul, that you have lost your 'joie de vivre'. You just don't seem the same Zoe.'

'Tia's right. We are a bit worried about you Zoe. You know you can talk to us. So?' Mel urged as Tia nodded.

'Well actually you are both right,' Zoe replied as she fussed with her napkin on her knee. 'Ok here goes. I will tell you everything. It will do me good to get it off my chest so to speak. So, when I was in Istanbul I felt rotten so I left Damianos and Michalis to the shopping while I stayed in bed in the hotel. Finally they returned with a load of leather goods. Anyway to cut a long story short, when we were coming back into Greece, Damianos told me to take a leather jacket and a pair of leather trousers through customs and made me wear his other new

A Lock up on Crete

leather jacket which looked ridiculous on me.' Zoe took a sip of the ice cold wine then continued.

'I couldn't refuse, as after all he had paid for the trip for me. But the customs officer took my passport and wrote in the back of it. I'll show you when we get back tonight. He said that when I returned to the UK I would have to declare them to customs. Anyway I wasn't too bothered but then when we got back to Ierapetra, Damianos took my passport, took a pen to it and changed the number 2 to a number 1. The worst thing is it looks so obvious.'

'Hang on,' Tia asked. 'Are you actually taking these leathers back home with you?'

'No they belong to Damianos and besides he's already sold them so if I do get questioned about them I'm in a right pickle. See what I mean now?' Zoe looked towards the island of Spinalonga in the distance as Mel took her hand.

'Ahh, no wonder you've been worried,' soothed Tia as she absently threw some bread to the fish in the water.

'Exactly.' Zoe sighed, freeing her hand to join in feeding the silver, darting fish.

'But why did Damianos change the number 2 to a 1?' Tia's brow furrowed as she straightened her back into the chair and stopped feeding the fish.

'He said that when I go through customs it would be better if it said I had to declare just one rather than two jackets,' Zoe explained raising her eyes. 'Oh I know it was a stupid thing to do and only highlights that I have something to declare.'

'Hang on. I assume it's written in Greek?' Mel added.

'Yes it's all written in Greek,' Zoe confirmed.

A Lock up on Crete

'Well how many UK customs officials are going to be able to read Greek? Hey I bet there's not one. It will be fine. Forget about it Zoe. There's nothing you can do.' Mel assured her with a slight hesitation in her voice.

Mel raised her brows to Tia as they changed the subject. 'This restaurant is divine. Imagine what it's like in summer. I bet it's heaving,' Mel continued as she scooped up a chunk of monkfish from her plate. The three friends agreed that the restaurant and setting was exquisite and was glad they had taken the extra bus ride from Agios Nikolaos to the quintessential fishing village of Elounda.

'And how did you enjoy the monkfish ladies,' the waiter asked as he cleared their plates away.

'Amazing,' they chimed, drinking in his good looks and trim body. An older man brought some baklava and ice cream.

'On my house ladies. Are any of you driving today?'

'No we are bussing it,' Zoe answered, directing his eyes to the two empty carafes of wine they had readily consumed. 'I mean we are taking the bus,' she added realising his confusion.

'Then allow me to share with you my family Raki. I am Spiro by the way and this is my restaurant.' From behind his back he produced a small carafe and four shot glasses and poured a little of the clear liquid into each. Placing each glass in front of the girls and one for himself he offered a toast.

'Yammas, good health,'

'Yammas,' they repeated in unison.

A Lock up on Crete

The girls didn't venture anymore that day, quite content to drink in the atmosphere of the restaurant and the surrounding beauty. They invited Spiro to sit with them as he questioned them about why they were in Crete out of season and offered them an insight into why they should visit Elounda in the spring and summer. They listened intently as the slight breeze moved them closer indoors and Spiro ordered hot chocolate all round with a little glug of Metaxa.

'Elounda is beautiful all year round as you can imagine. If you become bored of Iraepetra why don't you think about working here when the tourist season starts? I like to employ at least a few Brits during the busy season. I feel it helps with communication for the less confident tourists. Bill is English over there,' Spiro pointed to a slim man in paint splattered white overalls. He was balancing precariously on a ladder, leant on the pharmacy signage. 'Oh, I think he was in Iraepetra the other day,' Mel said as Spiro shouted across the way to Bill.

'Bill, Bill. Ella, ella. Come and have a rest.' As Bill turned around he nearly lost his footing on the ladder as the girls gasped. Knowing too well that Spiro's offer was more a demand, Bill placed the top on the paint pot and strolled over to where the girls had taken up residence for the afternoon.

'Bill. Please allow me to introduce my new friends from England.'

'Actually, one from Scotland,' Tia added with a mock frown.

'Ahh forgive me agape mou. Katsi katsi (sit) Bill. You must be tired now of all that paint.'

A Lock up on Crete

Bill did as he was told before recognising Mel and Tia from the taverna in Ierapetra.

'And so we meet again,' Bill said. 'I thought I recognised you two when you got off the bus earlier.' Spiro filled the shot glasses for another toast. Understandably, all four of them except Spiro, shuddered as the Raki assaulted their throats and seared through their insides.

'Better lay off that if you want to get back up your ladder,' Mel chuckled as Bill was about to take another slug.

'Yes. It is Sunday after all. I usually sit right here where we are now keeping Spiro entertained. Don't I Spiro?'

'Yes he does and empties my Metaxa bottle in return for English jokes! Last Sunday he was telling me of a girl he met in Iraepetra who makes the best bakewell tarts!' Spiro winked at Bill realising this was the English girl who Bill had enthused about last Sunday.

'Yes Bill used to be a baklava man and now all he can talk about is bakewell tarts and apple pies. You are now a competitor Mel,' Spiro teased with a hint of truth.

'Oh no I didn't realise. I thought it was just the locals in Iraepetra that bought my baking.'

Mel shifted a little in her seat and excused herself to go to the toilet. Bill and Spiro turned to Zoe and Tia as Bill explained.

'I was in Iraepetra on a little bit of a mission for the ex-pats of Elounda. Mel's boss has been advertising Mel's English baking to the wider ex pat community here and in Agios Nikolaos and it's taken off a storm. So on behalf of the ex-pats, who of course I am one, I went to check out if it really was an English girl who was baking them

A Lock up on Crete

and her boss wasn't importing them in. But don't tell Mel.' Bill revealed as both girls tried to act normal as Mel returned from the toilet. Mel seemed more composed as she sat back down and informed them the bus was leaving in half an hour. Before Bill resumed his painting, he left them a business card with the name of a taverna bar in Elounda which was frequented by a few ex pats, including him.

'If you are down in Elounda again, please give me a call,' he said scribbling his name and number on the card. 'Us ex pats are not as self- righteous as we are made out to be. Not here in Crete anyway.' With that remark, Bill shook their hands and walked back to his ladder across the quiet main road.

'Well girls, it is a pleasure to have spent a quiet Sunday with you. Now you come back soon and bring some of this famous tart of yours,' remarked Spiro as he kissed each girl on each cheek.

'Koritsis -Girls. Before you leave I translated your names,' he added turning to each girl in turn.

'Zoe means life. Melissa means honey and Tia is a goddess.'

'Thank you Spiro. We didn't know that. See you soon.' The three girls smiled at each other as they made their way to the bus stop.

Mel

The three friends had made a pact before they left for their winter adventure. The pact they had readily agreed upon was that they were to hold no secrets from each other, especially if it jeopardised their well- being. So a few days after their trip to Elounda, Tia and Zoe imparted the information that Bill had divulged about the marketing of her baking to the ex-pat community. Mel hadn't been too surprised; she had sensed the locals resentment too many times when her boss had shown them through to the kitchen where Mel baked. She felt the older women's antipathy and noticed their scowls as she diligently carried on baking. And then there was the incident at the taverna she mistook for her local taverna, when the waitress quizzed her about being the English baker.

In their defence, they probably felt she had invaded their territory, bringing her English
baking to a country renowned for desserts.

When all said and done, British and Greek baking were worlds apart and there really was no cause for concern. Mel reminded herself to put her boss out of his misery and reveal that she knew how he marketed her baking. She was more than happy to feed the bellies of the ex-pats who yearned for some British bakewells and tasty tarts. After all, it had brought Bill to Iraepetra and after the letter she had received that morning from Yannis, quite frankly she needed a distraction.

The letter from Yannis

A trip to the post office was always quite exciting for the three girls. That morning it was Mel's turn to pick up any mail. By now the post office clerks knew the girls well and allowed them to collect each other's mail. There was also the chance that Cara may have written to them.

A Lock up on Crete

However, there had only been one letter and that was for Mel.

Back in the kitchen, she opened the letter as a black and white photo fell out between the paper. It was Yannis and another male in uniform with their arms draped around each other. Yannis was beaming into the camera and she recognised the other smiling male but couldn't quite place him. He didn't look Greek that was for sure.

Dear Melissa mou,

I hope you are well and still in Iraepetra reading this letter. Firstly, I am sorry I didn't say goodbye after you left Agios Nikolaos without me. The truth is I was angry from a discussion with my aunt Apollonia. I told her she was wrong to accuse you girls with the silly bank note problem. She is not a good person and although she is family I don't want to know her and I feel she is to blame for us not saying goodbye to each other. Secondly, I wanted to tell you but couldn't find the right words so like a coward I am telling you on paper. I think maybe you know already and I didn't want you to think you are not desirable to me in an intimate sort of way because I think you are a beautiful person and an amazing friend. Melissa mou - the man in the photo is my boyfriend. He is from England and is serving with the Air Force in Cyprus. I met Ricky some years ago and we love each other. I hope you are not angry with me and I hope you write back. Nobody knows back home so please keep it between me and you or as you English say – mum is the word.

A Lock up on Crete

Lots of love from Cyprus
Your friend Yannis xxx

Mel studied Ricky's tanned features and dark hair which would have been curly if it had not been cut so short again and knew it was the Ricky she first thought it was. Although Yannis had asked for her to keep it private, she had to tell the girls.

'It's definitely him,' Mel confirmed as she showed the girls the photo of Yannis and Ricky that evening at the apartment.

'Sorry, but who do you think it is with Yannis?' asked Zoe as she dried her hair with a towel.

'You remember me saying I came out here four years ago with a girl called Rosie?'

Both girls nodded as Mel carried on. 'It's her ex fiancée, Ricky. Yannis boyfriend.'

'Oh wow! Did you ever meet him?' Tia asked as she sat up straighter in her bed.

'No, but Rosie showed me a photo of them as she announced her engagement. He must have been away on duty elsewhere. And then suddenly a month later she asked me if she could come to Crete with me. I never really questioned her engagement as I thought Ricky must have been overseas too. It's him for sure. Apart from the same name I remember focussing on his nose in the photo. In fact I had to stop myself from saying something about how his nose looked like a Greeks.' Mel recalled.

'I wonder if Rosie knew Ricky was gay then and that's why she came here with you to get over it?' asked Tia who was clearly intrigued by the story. 'Do you keep in touch with her?

'No, we seemed to lose contact after she left Crete. I assumed she had gone back to university. I could find out though.' Mel leafed through her frayed address book as Tia urged her to not to give up – she loved anything like this and didn't hold back when it came to piecing together puzzles of people's lives.

Suddenly Mel's eyes widened in the dimming light of the apartment kitchen.

'What is it Mel?' enquired Tia.

'Oh my Lord! Could it have been him?'

'Who? Who Mel?' asked Zoe, joining in.

'The pension in Heraklion. I haven't told you yet.'

'Oh my God Mel. Spit it out please!' chorused Tia and Zoe.

'Four years ago, when I was with Rosie in Heraklion, she was working on the grapes one day while I was cleaning the pension. It was the day that I found my Yannis with a male in bed when I let myself in to clean their room.'

'Mel! You didn't tell us that!'

'Well I'm still not 100% sure it was him to be honest but there again it must have been. It was the tattoo that gave it away. The small tattoo above his backside.' Mel smiled as she reminded Tia to close her mouth which was hanging on to her every revelation.

'I saw the same tattoo a few days ago when Yannis and I were on our trip. We stayed over in a taverna after an impromptu party. I woke up on the floor and a few metres away, there lay Yannis with his bare backside on view, cuddled up to another person! I assumed in my hung over state that it was a woman as the hair was longer and the sheet covered their body. But it must have been a male! A male with longer hair. Yes that male with a ponytail who I spotted the evening before on the dance floor!'

'Don't stop. Carry on,' Tia urged as she poured Mel a glass of water.

'That's when I subconsciously recognised the tattoo. So when we arrived in Heraklion, I couldn't believe it when we passed the pension I worked at with Rosie. And come to think about it, when I told Yannis I was there the four years previous, I noticed he flushed and said that he had been in Heraklion at the same time. So it really was him I barged in on and also now I am thinking the other male could well have been Ricky! Oh my God, poor Rosie! Now it all makes sense. She was so eager to leave Heraklion and she did mention that she was looking forward to meeting up with Ricky there but he had never shown up.' Mel took a sip of water as Zoe surmised.

'So maybe this Ricky guy had been there! In the pension but with Yannis! He must have been there to surprise Rosie, met Yannis somewhere along the way and ended up in bed with him!'

Tia interjected as Mel took a deep breath.

'So after their meeting in Heraklion, Yannis and Ricky must have kept in touch and now they are an item. Wow this just gets juicier. But Mel, how can you be sure it was Ricky in the pension and not some other male. Yannis sure is a dark horse!'

'I remember in those fleeting moments when I was riveted to the spot after letting myself in, Yannis' tattoo

and the image of the other male as he woke and turned to me. He mumbled something like *excuse me* in a clipped English accent. Oh and it was his nose.' Mel reached for the photo again and studied the image of Ricky as the girls waited eagerly for confirmation.
'Yes! Yes. It was definitely Ricky,'
'Well, well, well. At least it was you who caught them and not Rosie. And at least Yannis and Ricky can stop living a lie about their sexuality and be happy together.' Zoe reasoned as she bid the girls good night and urged them to do the same as they shuffled over to their respective beds.
'Kala nichta you two.'
'Night Night,' chimed Mel and Tia.

Zoe and Damianos

Zoe hadn't slept at all when the light filtered through the thin curtains the next morning. The thought of another day stood at that metal framework directing cucumbers up the conveyer belt through the wrapping machine, was totally mind numbing for her. The only consolation was that the money was quite good and at least she got to chat briefly with the Dutch couple and the two guys from Egypt. Without them, she felt she would go crazy to the point of screaming the factory down while throwing cucumbers at the Greek grannies.

Despite her reluctance, she dressed in her scruffs and headed down to the corner of the street where she waited for the pickup truck. No doubt Damianos would be in the front seat and simply nod his head in acknowledgement. She really wished he didn't work

A Lock up on Crete

there – it was awkward and there were no smiles from him at work-she was just another employee.

Ever since she had politely refused his offer to live at his, he had changed his attitude.

On a brighter note, it was payday and she intended to treat herself to some new jeans as the weather was turning wintry. She might also ask Tia if she could go to the salon and have a good haircut. After all, Tia could cut her hair at the apartment but going to the salon would show her boss just how good she was. She might even tell Tia that she could cut it into a graduated bob and really show off her expertise.

The day at the factory had gone surprisingly fast but Zoe hated having to clock watch – it was akin to wishing your life away. She was just getting ready to follow the others out for lunch and had switched the machine off, when Damianos appeared.

'Zoe I don't want you to talk to those touristees. You are becoming lazy at the job.'

Zoe was dumbstruck. She couldn't believe him. He might be her supervisor but she wouldn't tolerate following his demands, especially ridiculous ones like that. Thankfully she found her voice.

'Don't you tell me who I can speak to! In fact I hardly have time to look at them never mind engage in conversation. You are ridiculous prancing up and down like you own the joint.' Zoe knew that she had said too much as she felt the cold metal of the machinery slam into the side of her head. Her head was swimming with stars as she slumped to the cold floor as Damianos

A Lock up on Crete

walked away. The factory owners had witnessed the whole scene. In a matter of seconds, Costas was by her side and his brother Vasilis went in search of Damianos.

'Zoe, Zoe,' Costas urged as he felt her pulse and placed a large sponge under her head. In that split second from falling to hearing her name she wondered to herself why the Greeks seemed to repeat most things twice. Then, the next voice she heard as she lay on the concrete floor was the soft female voice of Costas's daughter.
'Zoe, I am Alexa, Costas's daughter. Can you hear me?' she pleaded. Zoe nodded.

Fortunately, Alexa had just returned from university in Athens where she was studying to become a nurse. She had only just arrived in town to surprise her father as she walked to the office door and spotted her father with Zoe.
'I don't think you have any injuries but I want you to go to the pharmacy if you feel any worse please. I will check with Papa tomorrow and ask how you are. Now go home but please try not to sleep until a few hours and until your friends are there with you. Papa will drive you to your apartment now. 'Alexa helped her to her feet as Costas brought his car to the side door. She caught sight of Damianos, held in a head lock by Vasilis, at the side of the road as he had tried to make his escape to the olive groves.

'What the hell! The bastard!' yelled Tia as she arrived back at the apartment. Word had quickly travelled to the salon about the incident at the cucumber factory. The moment she heard her friend's name mentioned she flew out of the salon back to the apartment.

'Why did he do that to you? The jealous bastard!' she added as Mel flew through the door.

'Zoe I've just heard Damianos hit you and you smashed your head into a machine. Jesus, what a malaca! How's your head? Should we take you to the hospital?'

Zoe sat up in bed and assured her friends that Alexa had checked her over and if she felt any pain or dizziness she was to go to the pharmacy.

'That's not good enough. You should have a bump to your head. Here let me take a look,' Tia insisted. 'I did my nurses training too.'

'Oh wow Tia, what other skills have you under your belt? It's surprising that although we are good friends we don't really know about each other's past. I reckon we have an evening where we each talk about our past, censored stuff too!' suggested Mel as she searched with Tia for a visible bump on Zoe's head.

'Ahhh there it is, just a tiny little bump but it's a bump and that's a good sign. It's a wonder the fall didn't break the skin. I have to admit, although it shouldn't have happened in the first place, you have been lucky. Wait till I tell Andreas about this. He will want to break Damianos's legs,' Tia hissed.

'No doubt he will know already Tia. I found out an hour after it happened and you did at the salon,' Mel said, rummaging in her bag for some mints for Zoe.

'Actually, Andreas is back in Agios Nikolaos to finalise the date for the will,' Tia explained.

A Lock up on Crete

'Maybe it's for the best,' whispered Mel as Tia followed her into the small kitchen to put the kettle on.

That night Tia and Mel took it in turns to watch over Zoe as she slept soundly. Maria had also insisted that Tia take the following day off to look after her friend. It still amazed her how well she had slotted in to life in Iraepetra with Andreas and his family. She too had had a proposal from Andreas to move in with him and his family. She had politely declined knowing that it was essential to keep their boundaries with the apartment and not to lose the closeness she had with Mel and Zoe. Andreas had been a little disappointed but understanding at the same time, hoping that one day he would spend as much time as possible with his wonderful wee Scottish girlfriend.

Throughout the next day, Tia periodically checked on Zoe, allowing her to rest up and drink plenty of fluids as they sat on the small balcony. Later in the afternoon they had a walk around the courtyard garden of the apartment until the rain started and they returned to their cosy kitchen. Tia decided to call Andreas while Zoe had a nap and was momentarily distracted by a soft knock at the door. It was Theo.

'Tia, Tia. I heard about the incident at the factory. How is Zoe? I do apologise as Damianos is a friend of mine but this does not excuse him for doing this. I have unfriended him. He is not one of us anymore.'

Tia assured Theo that Zoe was making a good recovery and would not be going anywhere near Damianos and the factory. Theo collected the rent while he was there

A Lock up on Crete

and told Tia to make sure they called him if Damianos came anywhere near the apartment.

Chapter 14

A few days later

'No Zoe. You can't go back to the factory. That's crazy. Look I will ask at Medusa's to see if they have any work for you,' Mel urged as Zoe pulled on her work clothes. Mel wished Tia was there to back her up and restrain Zoe from going to work at the factory but she had stayed over at Andreas's after him returning from Agios Nikoloas.

'It will be fine now. Alexa, the boss's daughter called me yesterday to check how I was and told me that Damianos had been sacked and that I could go back to work if I wanted to.'

'Well it doesn't seem as though I can stop you then does it Zoe? But if you feel dizzy or tired you get straight back here and call me at Medusa's,' Mel instructed as she handed Zoe her work number.

The work truck was waiting at the corner of the road as usual as Zoe speeded up her walk. She was greeted by her boss Costas as he motioned for her to sit in the passenger seat instead of with the women in the back . After a few pleasantries in broken English and Greek, they pulled in to the factory car park. It felt good for Zoe to be back. Despite the incident, her bosses, Costas and Vasilis had taken her side and had done their upmost to protect her. Zoe's happiness soon soured when she

A Lock up on Crete

spotted Damianos's mama moving her bulk out of the back of the truck.

During the morning, the machine worked non-stop and everyone was far too busy to gossip or even look around. Zoe was desperate for the toilet but as there was only the one toilet at the back of the factory next to the cucumber crate, it meant her having to budge past the Greek grannies and she could imagine the looks she would get from them.

No longer able to hold on, when the machine finally stopped for a quick maintenance, she darted to the toilet. After a long wee she opened the door and was greeted to a line of desperate women wriggling around for the loo. She couldn't help but smile as she passed them. She spotted Damianos's mama, who openly reciprocated her smile.

The few men who worked on the factory floor returned from a smoke and pee break in the field at the back and resumed their places as the machines roared into life again. The Dutch couple had placed themselves either side of Zoe to make sure she was fit to work, taking it in turns to keep her water bottle topped up. Gretel handed her a few mints to stave off the periods of boredom. Zoe wished she had brought some headache tablets with her as she felt a dull ache at the back of her head. She reminded herself to ask if anyone had any on the next break. Suddenly the machines fell quiet. Two policemen strode out of the office in the direction of the machine. The two Egyptian lads spoke rapidly to each other, jumped over the machine and fled it into the fields at

A Lock up on Crete

the back of the factory. The policemen didn't even make chase as they returned to the office opposite the machines with Costas and Vasilis. Zoe and the rest of the factory workers watched as they all took a seat and Costas handed the cigarettes round. Billows of cigarette smoke swirled around in the small office before escaping through the gap in the door. They could have almost been in a kafenion passing the time of day away as they threw their heads back in laughter. Eventually they left making eye contact with the touristees as they nodded their heads to each one of them in turn. Zoe shuddered and took a long gulp of air. Everyone seemed to hold their breath - the factory, now devoid of any human noise, emphasising the creaks and groans of the metal machinery. Vasilis and Costas strode across the factory floor.

'Please the three of you come into the office with me.'

'Coffee?' Costas asked as they took a seat in the smoke filled confines of the office.

All three touristees shook their head.

'Is it Damianos?' Zoe asked.

'The policemen were here because they had an anonymous call to inform them that we are employing touristees illegally. Usually they turn, what you say, a blind eye? For you three it means that you need to go to the police station later today but not all at the same time. You will need to take your passports. The policemen will tell you not to work again but you can return here in a week or so, no problem. You may have to give a little fine as we have had to,' Vasilis explained as Costas nodded in agreement.

A Lock up on Crete

'So why did the Egyptians run?' Gretel's boyfriend asked. 'Rumours say they were wanted back in Egypt. Of course they did not want to be known to the police here.' Vasilis said as a matter of fact as he shrugged his shoulders.

As they left the office, Vasilis motioned with his hand for Zoe to remain seated.

'Zoe. Stay away from him. It was Damianos who called the police. He was angry that we had sacked him after he pushed you into the machine.'

Zoe returned to the machine feeling she could throw up any minute. She reached for a mint in her pocket to relieve the awful taste building up in her mouth.

Iraepetra Police Station

Zoe was pleased to see the Dutch couple outside the police station as she thanked Costas for the lift back from the factory.

'Hello Zoe. We have shown the policeman our passport but we have decided to move on. We are going to Israel by boat. We hope to find a kibbutz to work and stay for a while.'

Gretel had a new sparkle in her eyes and her naturally blonde hair had escaped its bobble as she placed her passport in her handbag.

'I'm happy for you both. I will miss you though. And thank you for helping me and looking after me at the factory,' Zoe said with a lump in her throat.

'Stay away from him,' Gretel's boyfriend said to Zoe as he handed her a full bag of mints.

'Come on Hans. We need to catch the bus,' Gretel urged as she gave Zoe a tight squeeze.

A Lock up on Crete

Zoe watched them walk hand in hand until they disappeared from view. She turned to face the doors of the police station, took a deep breath and held her head high.

'Zoe Matthews. Your passport please?' the policeman asked in a gentle manner. She recognised him from the greenhouse shenanigans with the big lady. Any sign that he recognised Zoe was not apparent as he looked through her passport stopping at the last page.

'Zoe Matthews. Who wrote this?' he asked, pointing to the writing. Zoe felt the earth crumble beneath her.

'I went to Istanbul with Damianos and the border control wrote it in my passport,' she stammered.

'Damianos Kazantakis?' the policeman asked.

'Yes.'

'Po, po, po,' he replied raising his brows. 'Do you have two or one leather jacket?'

'I don't actually have any but it did say two originally,'

'So why is it changed from a 2 to a 1?'

'Damianos did it. He wrote over the number two to make it look like a number one.'

There was a new urgency as the policeman shouted for the relevant papers to be brought to him before instructing Zoe to write down a full statement of the passport incident.

The policeman returned two hours later with Damianos. As Zoe sat at the table outside the police officer's office, Damianos was ordered to remove all his clothing except for his underwear. There he stood, still wearing his watch and necklace until they too were taken away in a plastic pouch.

A Lock up on Crete

Zoe felt a pang of regret and sympathy. How had it gotten to this?

Another policeman took Damianos in handcuffs to a cell as the policeman focussed his attention on Zoe.

'Ok, Zoe. I am now going to hand you over to the tourist policeman. You can call him Tony or Adonis, whichever you prefer. He will be assigned to you throughout the proceedings. I take it you will want to press charges? Even if you don't feel you want to because of your illegal working, Costas the factory owner has made it clear that he will be pressing charges in court on Damianos Kazantakis for the assault at his factory on yourself.' His deep set eyes searched hers, searching her emotions.

Zoe felt relieved that she didn't actually need to press charges. Maybe Costas would drop the charges too if it all blew over. There again, Damianos had landed Costas and Vasilis a hefty fine for illegally employing the tourists. She wondered how far the two Egyptians had got to and who were they running from. She was shaken out of her reverie by Tony, her assigned tourist policeman.

'Zoe, please listen carefully. Are you feeling ok? I will send for water. Have you eaten?'

Zoe shook her head not recalling the last time she had eaten. The image of Damianos stripped of his clothes and possessions had made her feel sick.'

'I will have a small piece of bread please or a biscuit,' Zoe said, realising she must try to get something in her stomach. Suddenly she had to run to the toilet. Her insides were a volcano erupting with stress. The toilets were a mess which didn't help matters. She felt dirty and in need of a long hot shower.

On her return, Tony looked up from his paperwork and pushed a cold bottle of water and two plain biscuits towards her, realising she had either been sick or her bowels had reacted unexpectedly.

'When can I go home Tony?'

'Very soon Zoe. I need to ask you some more questions. Did Damianos Kazantakis offer you money to take these leather goods through the border?'

'No but he paid for my trip,' Zoe replied using all her strength and concentration to answer the question correctly in order to minimise both her and Damianos's wrongdoings.

'When you returned from Istanbul, were you ever with him when he sold the leather goods and if yes, did you witness any money exchange?'

'No, nothing at all,' Zoe answered honestly as she rubbed the side of her waist.

'Before you went on the trip to Istanbul, had Damianos Kazantakis treated you badly or ever swore at you?'

'Well he did swear a lot but obviously I didn't know exactly what it means in English. Also he has always been quite possessive but in a kind of good way,' Zoe informed Adonis, realising she had said too much.

'In what kind of good way Zoe?'

'Sorry I mean he has always helped me with work and his aunt was very kind to me after we returned from Istanbul. I had been ill and she nursed me back to health while Damianos worked and bought food for his aunt for me. She is a very kind lady.'

A Lock up on Crete

'Zoe. You are probably tired so just one more question then you can go.'

Zoe shifted uncomfortably in the chair as her head felt heavy and her stomach grinded and gurgled.

'We had reports which date back from a week before your trip. A neighbour saw a young tourist female trying to break free from Damianos Kazantakis outside his house. She was reported to run away with a plastic bag of clothes which spilled out onto the road. Damianos Kazantakis was seen to take the girl back to his house. The description fits you. Zoe. Was this girl you?'

Zoe wanted to flee right there and then. She hadn't told anyone, not even Tia and Mel about this incident. It was four in the morning and despite her screaming a couple of times she didn't think anyone would have witnessed it. She could sense that although she was trying to dumb down the incident, Damianos was in deep trouble already.

'Yes it was me,' she revealed as a tall, slim woman with dark bobbed hair similar to Zoe's entered the room.

'Ok Zoe. This is Anna, also a police officer. She will sit with you while you tell me what happened.'

'In your own time Zoe,' the striking policewoman soothed as she sat next to her.

'Ok it was nothing much and it all got out of hand. Damianos had asked if I wanted to start living with him in his room at the front of his parent's house. He said it would be cheaper for me rather than living with my friends at the apartment and paying rent. He said I could pay him a little bit of rent and it would help his parents as they are quite poor. I told him I would think about it

A Lock up on Crete

and stay over for a few nights before I made my mind up. I didn't really want to leave the apartment as I wanted to stay with my friends but he was very persuasive. So, after I told him my answer was no, he tried to keep me in his room. He even followed me to the toilet which was in a separate outside room.' Zoe took a sip of water, urged on by the Anna who had a soothing aura about her. Zoe continued, 'The next morning we both slept through the alarm as we had been arguing most of the night and so we missed work. Then again that night he wouldn't let me leave and locked his door from the inside and put the key in his pocket. Then, while he was sleeping that night, at about 3am I felt for the key but it wasn't in his jeans pocket which he had left on the floor. I then remembered there was another way out at the front which led onto a small garden. Damianos was snoring so I crept to the door and opened the shutter careful not to allow too much light in. I had my bag with a few overnight clothes in which must have alerted him as the plastic rustled. The door wasn't locked so I slid out. Within seconds he was chasing after me as I ran down the middle of the street. He took me back to his room after picking up my clothes that had spilled from the bag into the road.

'Take your time, Zoe. You are doing well,' Anna said as Zoe took another sip of the water. 'Eventually Damianos freed me the next day when his aunt asked about why he wasn't at work. I must say though, he didn't harm me physically.'

'Thank you Zoe. That will be all. You can go and get some sleep now and I will pay you a visit tomorrow.' The

A Lock up on Crete

interview ended abruptly as Anna guided Zoe to the front desk and discharged her.

'Please be careful Zoe. If you need to talk, you know I am here,' she assured her as they shook hands. Zoe walked the short distance to the apartment, feeling safe in the knowledge that Damianos was still in a cell but wretched that it had come to this.

Zoe objected the following day when Tia and Mel insisted they would take it in turns to stay with her, assuring them that Damianos was in a cell and the tourist policeman was checking up on her. Theo, their landlord was also staying around the apartment doing some small jobs. He felt enraged and naive that he too had been taken in by Damianos and his persuasive techniques. He felt it his duty as the landlord to keep his tenants safe. After all, he didn't want this incident to reflect on his personal character and lose him business. He prided himself on providing extremely comfortable rooms for long term tourists and had spent most of his compensation buying the run down apartments and renovating them to a very high standard. The only blow had been that his wife of twenty years had walked out of his life the day that the apartment block had been officially opened by the Mayor of Iraepetra. It was a week later that Theo discovered that it was the Mayor himself that she had been seduced by!

Tia and Mel reluctantly headed off to work, a little worried that they too may have a call from the police for working illegally.

A Lock up on Crete

Zoe assured them otherwise, repeating what Costas and Vasilis told her about the police usually turning a blind eye. Zoe wouldn't have been at all surprised if Costas and Vasilis had their fine waived already. It seemed like most people were trying to protect her from Damianos. What exactly had he done in the past? It must have been quite serious for him to gain notoriety in his home town. She might delve deeper and ask Tony, the tourist policeman later on when he called.

'Please Zoe do not worry. I cannot disclose to you about Damianos Kazantakis's past. Firstly, he is my cousin and secondly, after his court appearance I do not think he will ever break the law again. Zoe gasped as she took in the two statements. Surely Tony couldn't be involved with the case if they were cousins and secondly it had progressed now to a court hearing. She felt numb. 'Tony, have Costas and Vasilis decided on court action?' 'No they wanted to but they think that it will start a lot of ill feeling around Iraepetra and will only bring it to the attention of the court that they employ illegally. But because you have broken the law by working you are required to press charges or it will be worse for you. I am sorry if you didn't want to but I have been instructed by my superior that you must or may have to leave Crete.' Tony placed his hand on her shoulder. Zoe's heart, followed swiftly by her stomach, plummeted to the ground. 'Oh hell! I feel awful. Damianos is his own worst enemy. If only he wasn't so possessive.'

A Lock up on Crete

'Zoe unfortunately this is an undesirable trait for the minority of Greek men. We are born with a lot of love but we are also born with an inherent jealousy too. Some of us more than others. We call it Zilia or refer to our Greek mythology,' Tony explained.

'Oh I am intrigued now. What is this Greek mythology?' Tony sighed, wishing he hadn't mentioned it, then began.

'In Greek mythology the God of jealousy and envy is Phthonos, the personified spirit Daimon. I remember when my cousin was born. I was about ten years of age. I heard my mama saying to my papa that her sister had given her baby a cursed name and she would persuade her to change Damianos's name. Obviously it didn't happen and the curse had gotten Damianos!'

Tony stayed for another coffee then made his way to the door where Theo was clearing up the wood shavings he had been planing from the door opposite.

'Kalimera ' Theo nodded to Zoe as he followed Tony down the stairs.

Chapter 15

Mel, Elounda

'Tia, are you sure Zoe will be ok?'

'Yes of course Mel. Just get yourself off to Elounda. It's about time you had some fun!' Tia remarked as they sat on their balcony after making sure Zoe was asleep.

'What do you mean Tia?' she asked, a little perplexed.

A Lock up on Crete

'Well you know. All that with Yannis.'

'All what?'

'The trip he took you on and then all that with sending you a photo with him and his lover. By the way, did you get a reply from Rosie, Ricky's ex?'

'No. I decided not to get in touch with her. Water under the bridge, so they say. I was just glad that it was me who found them together and not poor Rosie. I'm sure Ricky would have called off their engagement gently though and who knows she may never find out that he bats for the other side! And as long as he makes Yannis happy, I'm happy.' Mel added as she painted her toe nails with a bright orange colour.

'Well you didn't know Yannis was gay, did you?'

'Oh Tia we were only ever good friends anyway and there were plenty of clues along the way. I'm tired to be honest. I think I'll go to bed if you don't mind.'

Tia knew she had gone too far as she attempted to lighten the mood.

'Let that fluorescent nail varnish dry first Mel,' she smiled as Mel's lips made an o shape before she pretended to throw the varnish at her friend.

'Night Tia, sleep well.'

'Night Mel, yes you too.'

On the way to Agios Nikolaos, Mel reflected on the past few days. She was glad when she had picked up her mail the day before and received a short letter from Bill in Elounda.

Hey Mel,

A Lock up on Crete

*Remember me Bill? The daft ex pat painter in Elounda.
I'm a bit slack at work so I was wondering if you would
like to bring me over a bakewell tart or any tart for that
matter on your next day off. I could meet you at Agios
Nikoloas bus station. I have a rickety scooter and we
could zoom back to Elounda and I will show you the
sunken city of Olous. Here is my number just in case you
lost it.*
Hope to hear from you.
Bill
x

Mel had asked for the day off as her boss was very
flexible with her shifts. She even offered to take some
baking with her to drop off at the ex- pat taverna in
Agios Nikolaos. She cleared her throat as she waited for
Bill to answer. Not one for phone calls, she blurted to Bill
that she would be at Agios Nikolaos bus station the next
day at 11am. Bill sensed her reluctance to make small
talk on the phone so finalised the arrangements with a
pleasant - *'see you soon.'*
The bus to Agios Nikolaos had been held up with goats
and sheep in the road. It was quite a sight as Mel
listened to the farmer yelling at them in a sing song voice
with the echoes of the tinkle of their bells in the
distance.
Bill was waiting beside his red and white rickety scooter.
She noticed he had a spare helmet.
'Hey Bill. How are you?' she said as she set foot on the
pavement.
Hey, Mel. I'm good now. How are you?'

A Lock up on Crete

'Yes I'm glad to see the Britishness in you bringing a spare helmet. Safety first!'
'Abso bloody lutely!' Bill grinned.

After Mel hitched up her maxi skirt and hopped on to the scooter they rode along in silence. The vivid turquoise sea of Mirabello Bay twinkled beneath them, enticing them along the quiet coast road.
Twenty minutes later they arrived at the small canal which opened into the bay of Elounda.
'So did you bring me my tart?' Bill asked as he parked his scooter near the sea wall.
'Oh My God! I don't believe it. I have forgotten everything. I've left them all in the apartment. My boss will be livid!'
'Good grief. How many did you fetch me Mel,' Bill asked puzzled.
'I said I would deliver a full batch of tarts for the taverna opposite the bus station to save him the journey. I left them all in the apartment.' Mel paced up and down the small bridge over the narrow canal.
'Can you call him? Put your mind at rest. Then you can enjoy the rest of the day,' Bill suggested, hoping that they could resume their date sooner rather than later.
'No. I'll foot the bill myself. I'll pretend I delivered them. I don't want to make a fool of myself. Sorry about your tart Bill.'
Bill's eyes crinkled at the side as he directed Mel to the side of the bridge.

'Sit down Mel. Have a minute. Right ok, so I gather from your last trip to Elounda you were itching to find out more about the history.' Bill started.

'Oh, was I?'

'You were looking at the paper place mat with the map of the area,' Bill winked.

'Ah yes I am a bit of a map freak. I used to read the A to Z of Lancaster, up north.'

'Whoa! Heavy duty Mel. Could you not afford comics?'

'Cheeky sod,' Mel quite enjoyed the quick northern banter with Bill, one thing she could actually say that she missed about home.

'Whether you like it or not, let me impart my knowledge on you Miss Lancaster.'

'Hey how do you know I'm from Lancaster?'

'I'm an accent expert,' he replied yet with another wink.

'So, if you cast your eyes down to the water here, this is the ancient city of Olous.'

'Oh wow, yes I can see the uniform stones. Go on,' urged Mel as she knelt down for a better view.

'The people who lived here were in conflict with the citizens of Dorian Lato until a peace treaty was eventually reached. Elounda was under the rule of the Venetians. The bulk of the city of Olous was reclaimed by the sea towards the end of the ancient Greek period. If it was summer we could have snorkelled and seen more,' Bill explained giving Mel a little nudge with the suggestion.

'Yeah I'd be up for that,' Mel knelt closer to her new ex pat friend, genuinely interested in the little history lesson.

A Lock up on Crete

'Then during the early 1900's, Elounda acted as a stopping off point for lepers being transported to the leper colony of Spinalonga. Can you see Mel? That island over there.'

'Yes I can see it. Oh wow! I remember trying to find Spinalonga when I was here four years ago and I walked from Agios Nikolaos a few miles following the beach front and thought I was in Elounda,' Mel raised her eyebrows and shrugged her shoulders.

'You great numpty!' Bill laughed as he composed himself to relay the next part of the history. 'Then in the 1930's these waters up to the peninsula past Spinalonga was used by the Imperial Airways flying boats as a landing to refuel when they were flying long range to the Middle East. And that Miss Lancaster as in Lancaster bomber, is about it in a nutshell.'

'Well thank you for that little history lesson. I'd love to go to the leper colony actually,' Mel said as she cast her gaze towards the gentle hump of the island.

'Unfortunatley, there are no boats in the winter but hop on the old girl and I'll take you even closer.'

A few miles down the road they reached the tiny village of Plaka. Bill cut the engine to the scooter as he took Mel's shoulder and guided her along to the edge of the tiny concrete pier where a solitary fishing boat bobbed up and down on the choppy water.

Five minutes passed in silence as they gazed in awe out to the former leper colony of Spinalonga. Mel felt as though she could reach out and touch it and like a dolls house, explore the cross sectioned houses that now had been left in disrepair and walk along the cobbled streets.

'It's incredible. I can feel a magnetic pull towards it. Can you imagine what it must have been like for the poor lepers?'

'Unbelievable. And it was only closed as a leper colony as late as 1957. And there was still no cure for it.' Bill contemplated slipping his arm around Mel as she hung on to his words. Suddenly, Mel straightened up as though she had just come to a realisation.

'It's a comical name –Spinalonga. It doesn't really sound Greek, does it?'

'You're right Mel. it doesn't sound Greek at all. In fact Mel, when the Venetians ruled they renamed it after an island near Venice of the same name. *Spina* meaning *Thorn* and *Longa* meaning *Long* – they must have thought it looked like a long thorn sitting in the bay.' Bill tilted his head in agreement with himself as he looked at the lonely island across the choppy waters.

'This is uncanny,' Mel exclaimed.

'What's uncanny?'

'That is my surname.'

'What? Your name is Melissa Spinalonga?' Bill asked with a quizzical look.

'No silly! I am Melissa Longthorn!'

'No way! So the island of Spinalonga really takes its name from you Miss Lancaster, Spinalonga, Longthorn!' Bill squeezed Mel's arm and Mel reciprocated as they drank in the image of the island opposite them.

A Lock up on Crete

They rode back to Elounda and then on to Agios Nikolaos in silence as Mel felt a pull towards this friendly ex pat as she gently rested her chest in the hollow of his back.

'Well Miss Lancaster, I mean Miss Spinalonga, I mean Miss Longthorn, I do hope you enjoyed your little trip out today and I hope we can meet up again. I have plenty of little gems like Spinalonga and Plaka up my sleeve that I can take you to.'

Mel thanked Bill profusely as she pecked him on the cheek and bought her ticket from the kiosk for the last bus to Iraepetra.

'Hey, next time I will remember to bring the tart,' she called back to Bill as she pulled herself up the steps of the bus.

'I'll hold you to that. Safe journey Mel.' Bill blew her a kiss as he waited until he lost sight of the incredible flame haired northern lass.

Chapter 16

Andreas, Ierapetra

Andreas was fuming. He regarded himself a proud Cretan with upstanding morals and upheld the filoxenia ethos of his country. He did not take too kindly to fellow Cretans who let the side down.

Like the majority of the population of Ierapetra, he knew of the Kazantakis family and the notoriety of a few members, notably Damianos and his Aunt Apollonia, the trouble causer. He knew he should have divulged his thoughts to Tia when he first met her outside the toilets in the bar. He had already heard snippets of conversation coming from the male toilet. It was unmistakenly the voice of Damianos speaking to someone about his next conquest. *'The girl in the bar. She has dark hair and striking blue eyes and is wearing a cream dress. She's my next conquest.'*

Andreas had meant to keep an eye on the situation but Tia had fortunately bumped into him on exiting the ladies and he was rooted to the ground. And then it became fuzzy - Tia and her beauty; too many drinks; realisation that Damianos had left the bar and Tia's friend was nowhere to be seen. He woke up the following morning with a horrendous hangover but with sublime images of the beautiful Tia etched forever in the lids of his eyes.

Andreas decided to set a few hours aside from his work schedule to visit the tourist policeman and ask if he could help in anyway.

As he envisaged, Adonis the tourist policeman who he knew was Damianos's cousin, could not impart too much information. He warned Andreas not to take matters into his own hands; after all, they didn't want a repeat of the notorious family feuding a few years earlier which resurfaced in Iraepetra, resulting in two near fatatlities. 'Please Andreas. Do not get involved too much. If you can keep an eye on Zoe and report back to me anything unusual. We do not need a repeat of the Irish girl, Andreas?'

Andreas returned to work, mulling over what Adonis had advised. He vaguely remembered an Irish girl.

A Lock up on Crete

Theo

Theo also prided himself on his 'filoxenia' It was an integral part of being a Cretan and a Greek national. He felt betrayed by Damianos. Damianos had been a huge help over the years he had to admit. For a favourable commission, Damianos would direct tourists to Theo's apartment block a short walk from the main seafront eateries. However, he knew of his family and their negative reputation but as in most families, it was usually a few members that spoiled it for the rest. Apart from the older spinster, Apollonia, the rest of the family kept out of trouble. Damianos had unfortunately showed his true colours with this incident with Zoe and had marred the family reputation even more so. It was hard to imagine that the tourist policeman, Adonis was the cousin of Damianos. He wondered how awkward that may turn out if Adonis had to testify against his own cousin. Theo told himself that it was his duty as a reputable landlord and Cretan that he would protect all his tenants, in particular the three English girls or rather the two English and one Scottish as Tia often reminded him with the same amount of annoyance and bonhomie. They were good tenants thus he decided to supply them with a decent heater in preparation for the vagaries of the Cretan winter. They were quite lucky in the south coast of the island for the long sunny summer months but the winters could take on a mind of their own and throw at them storm after storm with the occasional hailstones as large as tennis balls. Despite the sometimes harsh weather, Theo knew he lived in one of the best parts of Greece and never took it for granted – he just wished his beautiful wife hadn't been succumbed to the smarmy advances of the Mayor. Fortunately he didn't see them around town as they spent a lot of time in Heraklion at their sumptuous villa, funded no doubt by the residents of Iraepetra!.

Andreas and the hearing of the Will of the late Manolis Mariakis - Agios Nikolaos, December 1984

Although Tia had offered to accompany Andreas to the final hearing of the Will of his late uncle, he thanked her but asked if she could look after the salon in order that his sister Maria could attend. His parents had also declined the offer to attend knowing full well that their son was more than capable of dealing with everything efficiently. Besides, they had an idea of the reading of the Will and were excited about what the outcome might mean for their children.

Andreas was absolutely dumbfounded when he walked with Maria into the lawyers for the reading of the Will. In the corner of the reception area, like an unwelcome visitor sat Apollonia, dressed in her black weeds as if she were the lawful widow of Manolis Mariakis. Andreas wished it was the previous lawyer he had dealt with for the reading of the will, but somehow his uncle had instructed a different one.

'What the hell is she doing here?' Maria hissed as they followed the lawyer into a separate office.

'I'm afraid that there have been some developments with your uncle's will. It seems the lady sat in reception has produced another will made by your uncle a week before his death.

Andreas and Maria felt the whole office swallow them up as they heard the lawyer but struggled to comprehend just exactly what the well-mannered lawyer was saying.

Chapter 17

Zoe and Damianos
Initial court hearing, Lassithi prefecture, Crete, December 11, 1984

Zoe had been taking long walks along the beach most days after the factory incident. Tony, the tourist policeman had been in touch every few days and had instructed her on the initial court hearing that she would have to attend before the main one. Her mind was clouded most of the time as she realised she should have really gone to hospital after the fall against the machine. A few painkillers usually sorted it but she wasn't so keen on relying on drugs. Maybe the stiff sea breeze may help her negative mood; she wondered if she could have done things differently to prevent Damianos acting the way he had. She talked her feelings through with Mel and Tia and it was the same answer – *no you didn't do anything wrong so stop beating yourself up about it.* She knew they were right as she honestly hadn't done anything devious. One of her downfalls had been her naivety about the trip to Istanbul and her compliance with the passport debacle.

The truth was, she felt embarrassed and ashamed of the whole affair and devastated that she would have to testify against Damianos. She didn't detest him and neither did she think he detested her. Unfortunately, he had allowed the green eyed monster to get the better of him, resulting in devastating and irreparable consequences.

She decided to head back to town as the wind had whipped up the waves and circled around her body, chilling her to the bone. It was Friday and she would have usually been looking forward to the weekend if she had still been working at the factory. Not wanting to go back to an empty apartment, she decided to call on the girls and pass a few hours away.

The first workplace she passed was the salon. Maria had left Tia in charge again.

'Hey Tia,'

'Oh hi, Zoe. Come on in from the cold. Go in the back and make a brew will you?'

The one customer had just left as Zoe handed her friend a steaming mug of tea.

'How's things?'

'Oh you know. Aimlessly wandering around. I miss the factory and all the noise, believe it or not,' Zoe revealed as she dunked a biscuit into her tea. Tia tilted her head to the side to elicit some truth, a mannerism of the Greek's she had soon adopted.

'I wish I had a few more hours to myself to be honest. I don't know what Maria finds to do but she's increasingly

A Lock up on Crete

'just popping out' and although my Greek is getting better with the customers, I can just imagine I'll make a huge mistake one day and cut their hair wrong or put the wrong colour on when my Greek and their English gets lost in translation. Both girls giggled as they imagined a Yiayia with a short back and sides and bright red hair.

Zoe's mood lifted as she swept the floor for Tia before leaving and checking in on Mel at Medusa's.

'Sorry Zoe. I send Mel home. Poor Mel she has huge head ache. So I send her home,' Mr M explained, handing her the last slice of Mel's apple pie the locals were now becoming addicted to and buying in droves. Zoe bought some more painkillers as she passed the pharmacy on the way back to the apartment. She felt a new pounding at the front of her head and wondered if like Mel, it was the change in air pressure that had given them both a headache. Mel was fast asleep as she entered the room. She poured herself a glass of orange, took two tablets and snuggled down into her bed. She wished it was Monday night and the preliminary hearing was over with.

The preliminary court hearing

The taxi picked Zoe up at 10 am on Monday morning. She was astounded to see Damianos in the back seat and another man whose once white shirt was now covered in splashes and streaks of red. His nose had taken an appearance of a watermelon and his hands were cuffed. Tony, the tourist policeman was nowhere to be seen as the man in the passenger seat in a black suit motioned her to get in the back. There was no other option but to sit next to Damianos as he was also forced to encroach on the other passenger's space.

The taxi sped away from Iraepetra and took the road inland. They passed the ubiquitous blankets of plastic that covered the landscape as they started to ascend into the mountains. Zoe wanted someone to speak. It was deathly quiet except for the radio blaring out Greek bouzouki music. The taxi was stifling as body odours and bad breath swirled around her nostrils. She looked to her right at Damianos. He stared straight ahead as a tear escaped his eye, followed by another one and then a whole stream of tears mixed with snot covered his face. Still he did not make eye contact with Zoe; it was as if he hadn't even noticed her. He looked dejected and a little unkempt as his usual contained curls sprang out in every direction.

They continued driving uphill, passing roadside bullet marked signs of pistols, directing drivers to pistol shooting venues. Zoe felt a shiver trickle down her spine and wanted to ask Damianos where they were heading. It was evident that this was no time for any communication. The handcuffed man next to him had fallen asleep on Damiano's shoulder - much to his dismay.

Finally, after an hour navigating hairpin bends, the taxi screeched into a driveway. The man in the passenger seat opened his door and stretched before indicating for Zoe and the others to follow him to a detached grey building.

A Lock up on Crete

Inside, the man in the suit presented his lawyer credentials to the unsmiling woman sat at a vast wooden desk. She nodded as she motioned them all through to the next room. A police officer took the passenger who had been sitting next to Damianos first. Ten minutes later, Damianos was called through as the other man returned and with the force of an elephant plonked himself in the seat next to Zoe. For a large room, Zoe wondered why they had to sit so close to each other. She inched her way to the next seat as he presented a toothless smile to her. Likewise, he inched his thin body next to her until she finally stood up and stood by the window.

Damianos returned with a slightly more confident air about him as he made eye contact with Zoe for the first time since she had been ordered into the taxi. Damianos took her seat as the man in the suit accompanied Zoe through to the room - she felt she was back in primary school again - going in to see the headmaster after a false accusation by another child. A stocky man with a thick moustache rose up slowly from his desk as if it was a major effort. Rather than offering her a chair, he walked round his desk to stand face to face with her. 'We need an answer,' he balled out in Greek. The man with a suit on translated.

'I don't know what you mean,' Zoe replied.

'What do you mean? Is it not simple enough?' he balled again never taking his stone eyes from hers. The man in the suit replied to the official but didn't translate. To Zoe, it seemed that he could have been asking the official for a little leniency on her behalf. The official

A Lock up on Crete

shrugged his shoulders and stared so hard it took Zoe so much willpower not to crumble.

'Why you cry like baby?'

'Because I'm still not sure what is happening,' Zoe explained as tried to stem a tear from trickling down her cheek. Her head pounded and beads of sweat began to form on her forehead as he waved them both out of the door. Thankfully, Damianos and the other man were already seated in the taxi. She quickly wiped her face and slid in next to Damianos as they returned to Iraepetra. The last few hours had felt surreal as she stepped out of the taxi at the apartment and the three remaining passengers continued to stare forward.

The rest of the day dragged as the rain lashed at the balcony door. She sat on her bed and hugged her knees. Eventually, after reading her latest crime novel, she welcomed the sound of the girls as they returned from work.

'It's like a bloody monsoon out there,' Tia remarked as she plonked herself on her bed and threw her wet clothes on the floor. Mel followed suit but carefully hung her soaked clothes on the make shift maiden in the kitchen.

'So how was it?' Mel enquired.

'Honestly, it was surreal in the fact that I haven't a clue why I had to go and why Tony, the tourist policeman wasn't there for me. I don't know where I have been and who I have given my passport details to. I honestly feel like I have dreamt it. I even had to sit next to Damianos in the taxi and another fella next to him looked like he'd

A Lock up on Crete

just had ten rounds with Mike Tyson with blood spattered all over his shirt. Then there was a man in a dark suit with a bowl shaped haircut in the front who translated for me but didn't introduce himself. I then had to go to a room where Damianos and the other bloke had been already and the horrid official made me cry and shouted at me when I couldn't stop. I honestly think I've been set up, especially when Damianos returned from seeing the official with a smirk on his face.' Zoe's cheeks glistened with moisture as her friends moved closer and put their arms around her shoulder. 'Damianos! Why was he there in the taxi?' Tia admonished as Mel leant over her bed and pulled a tissue from the box.

'I honestly don't know why they didn't keep us apart. On the way up there Damianos was bawling like a baby but now I know it was all for show. Jeez, I just hope I haven't been set up for something I didn't do,' Zoe took the tissue from Mel and blew her nose. Tia put on her jacket and took the umbrella from where it was drying off near the door.

'Where are you going Tia,' Mel asked her friend who was suddenly on a mission.

'I'm going to Andreas. He will shed some light on it. It all sounds very weird. Don't go anywhere you two. I'll be back soon,' On her way down the two flights of stairs she bumped into Theo.

'Hello Tia. Are you ok?'

'Oh hello Theo *etsi ketsi*, so so. How are you?'

'Yes or No?' he queried.

A Lock up on Crete

Tia blurted out what Zoe had told them realising straight away that maybe she shouldn't have. Theo nodded his head while pacing up the stairs.

'That was quick,' both girls said as Tia returned with Theo. Their caring landlord pulled up a chair and sat in the middle of the room.

'Let me explain,' he said, focussing his attention on Zoe. He continued to explain in as simple terms as possible how the Greek judicial system worked. The girls were relieved to find that everything had been in order and it had been the preliminary hearing that Zoe had attended. However, Theo also displayed his anger as to the way Zoe had been left in the dark and the way she had been intimidated by the official; who did have a reputation as being a bully.

'If I had known you would have to share a taxi with criminals I would have taken you myself,' Theo added as he pursed his lips and elicited a Pah, pah pah – a Cretan trait to display disgust, which the girls were now used to. 'Thank you Theo. I feel much better now and I should be able to sleep,' Zoe assured. Theo rose to leave and Mel accompanied him to the door. As usual, Theo had scanned the apartment, which to his delight was being kept immaculate, save for the heap of wet clothes on the tiled floor.

Chapter 18

Andreas

A Lock up on Crete

Andreas's infuriation with Apollonia and the contesting of the will was temporarily overshadowed with the Zoe/Damianos situation. If truth be told, he had never really liked Damianos and had kept his distance from him over their formative years. He had, since Adonis, the tourist policeman had mentioned it the other day, remembered the incident a few years back involving Damianos and an Irish girl. Andreas had been working near Chania on the west side of the island and when he returned it was basically old news but still enough news for the gossip mongers to share with each other. All he could recall was how Damianos had gone to Dublin with her to work in a Greek restaurant. Three months later they were back in Iraepetra with enough money to buy a rundown taverna on the outskirts of town towards Ferma. Rumour had it that the Irish girl fled back to Ireland over a piece of sentimental jewellery he had supposedly taken from her and the taverna was up for sale soon after. He would ask his mama what the exact story was before imparting anything to Tia.

Mel

It had only been one week since they had last met as Mel dialled Bill's number hoping to rendevouz again on her next day off. Bill didn't answer. Engulfed in disappointment she gave up after the fifth attempt that day. Maybe it was just as well he didn't answer as she needed to focus her attention and be with Zoe due to the impact of the recent events. She worried about the amount of headaches her friend seemed to be having; it seemed she was forever popping pills. Mel's primary

A Lock up on Crete

concern for her next day off was to spend with Zoe and work on her mental wellbeing. If only she could get her out of her pyjamas and out in the fresh air it would be a start.

Michalis

Michalis felt dreadful. He needed a good winter walk on the beach – that usually sorted his head out. As he pulled up on his scooter, he saw a familiar figure heading up the deserted beach. Her body was braced forwards in an attempt to fight the south easterly wind blowing in from the south Aegean Sea. Deliberating what to do for the best, he popped a coin into the vending machine outside the closed beach shop and opened up the carton of frappe. It was awful but it helped him gather his thoughts. He hadn't seen Zoe since all the trouble at the factory. Of course he had been in touch with Damianos who had confided in him about his possessive streak that had controlled his life for too long. Damianos needed help he had told him. Michalis was four years older than Damianos and knew less than most people about his chequered past. Although Michalis had been warned about the Kazatakis family he had witnessed a vulnerability about Damianos and had thus befriended him.

Michalis had wanted to study in Athens in psychology and become more than what his papa had in mind for him. Alas, on the premature death of his papa, he left school and continued the family business. If the souvlaki stall wasn't as revered and successful as it was, his life

A Lock up on Crete

might have turned out much different. However, he didn't have many regrets as his primary concern was to keep his mama with a decent roof over her head. He regarded himself too as quite a philosophical person, believing that people come into your life for a reason as Damianos had done and now Zoe. He had actually missed Zoe since the trip to and from Istanbul. From a spectator's point of view it could have looked that he was her boyfriend the way he cared for her during her illness. Plus, he would never have put a girlfriend in the position that Damianos had done with the leather jackets. He was utterly disgusted with his friend but had felt it his duty to reassure his friend and girlfriend that it would all sort itself out. But it hadn't! And now here was Zoe, seemingly in the same mood as him, walking their worries away on the arctic beach.

Instinctively, Zoe turned round and dug her feet in the sand as she faced the wind that had quickly gained speed from the swelling sea. She started walking towards Michalis, waving as she walked.

'Kalimera, Michalis,'

'Kalimera Zoe. What you doing on this cold winter day apart from battling in the wind?'

'Much the same as you by the looks of it,' she replied, sheltering under the canopy of the shop.

'I'm sorry I haven't been to see you,' Michalis said with his head slightly bowed. Zoe noticed his long eyelashes for the first time.

'Hey please do not apologise. It is awkward for us both but I have been pining for one of your souvlaki's,' she smiled.

A Lock up on Crete

'Ok we will go for one. Hop on the scooter.' Zoe loved being spontaneous as she threw her right leg over and grasped Michalis's slim waist.

Half an hour later they reached a small village where Michalis's school friend also owned a souvlaki stall. Zoe jumped off the scooter a little too eagerly as Michalis saved her from a face full of gravel as he threw himself onto her.

'You need a souvlaki that bad Zoe?' he laughed.

'Absolutley, it's the first time I have wanted to eat anything for days,' she replied, eyeing up the succulent pork, slowly gyrating on the stand.

'Well obviously, not ten out of ten like your souvlaki and gyros but I will give it a high nine.'

'You are biased I guess,' Michalis smiled as he continued to mop up the tzakiki with the last of his pita. It never failed to amaze Zoe how articulate in English the younger generation of Greeks were. It made her quite embarrassed sometimes that she and the majority of British people, failed to pick up their beautiful language.

'So now the awkward question,' Michalis said as his friend brought two small beers and set them on the small table beside them. 'When is the court case?' Michalis asked through clenched teeth.

'I'm not sure. A few weeks perhaps but if it is, I need to be doing something. The days are lonely when Tia and Zoe are working and my funds are running low. Do you know of any work Michalis?'

'Giannis,' he called over to his friend.

'Yes my friend,' he answered, dragging a chair up to Michalis. 'How can I help?'

A Lock up on Crete

'You know a lot of greenhouse owners around Iraepetra I'm sure. Do you know if any need a hard working English girl perhaps?'

'Not that I know but I will certainly ask for you. Here, write your number on this mat and I'll call you,' Giannis offered as he replenished the bottles of beer.

'Efcharisto poli – thank you,' Zoe said as she took out a few drachma notes to hand to Giannis.

'Oh put the money away – this is my treat. It is nice to see my friend with a twinkle in his eyes. You make him happy,' Giannis widened his eyes and waved his hand in the air.

'Good luck you two,' he added as Michalis started up his small scooter and freewheeled down the hill – a driving technique to save fuel that Zoe had noted many drivers did in Crete.

Michalis dropped Zoe off at the apartment as he reminded her about keeping in touch with Giannis for work.

The next evening there was a knock on the apartment door as all three girls stared at each other; they were not expecting anyone and it was quite late. Mel shuffled out of her bed and asked who it was before opening the door.

'It's Michalis. I need to talk to Zoe please.'

'Sorry but she is asleep,' Mel replied through the wooden door.

'It's ok Mel,' Zoe said as she joined her at the door. Mel moved over to allow Zoe to open the door.

'Zoe. Can you start tomorrow morning?' Michalis said as he fidgeted with his keys.

'Start what?' Zoe asked, careful not to allow him to enter the apartment.

'Oh sorry Zoe, I am not explaining myself at all well. Giannis called me this evening and I didn't take your phone number so that is why I am here in person. Giannis's friend needs a few days help in his greenhouse. It is just a short walk up from the beach where we saw each other the other day. Fotis has a Dutch wife who is very friendly and you will be working with her. It will be nice for you I am sure.'

'Yes. Of course I can. Thanks so much Michalis. I owe you one!' Zoe said, realising that the term – *I owe you one* was lost on him as he frowned then wrote the address of the shop where she was to meet Fotis the following morning at 7am.

'Is that Damianos's friend you went to Istanbul with? Tia asked with a quizzical frown.

'Yes we bumped into each other the other day and it was me that asked him if he knew of any jobs,' Zoe insisted.

'Fair enough but just be careful please,' added Mel.

'Don't worry I will. I'm looking forward to doing something constructive again instead of moping about in my pyjamas. At least I will be with this Dutch woman, a fellow northern European.' Zoe pulled the blanket closer to her chin.

All girls slept soundly despite the storm battering the town of Iraepetra.

A Lock up on Crete

Chapter 19

<u>Apollonia</u>
Apollonia was livid. Damianos, her nephew, needed her
and although he had a habit of finding trouble with the
tourist girls she loved him dearly. He was the youngest
of the family and she felt he had not had the affection
from her sister than his siblings had. She knew that
Katerina, his other aunt from his papa's side of the
family lived next door to them and kept her eye on him.
However, Katerina was not as astute as she was.
Apollonia wished sometimes she could live in Iraepetra
but she knew Agios Nikolaos was the better place to live
and work for her. Now though, she needed to visit her
birth town again and contact her nephew to find out
which one of the three touristee girls had landed him in
the police cell.

On the bus the following morning, she reflected on her
nephew's childhood, delving into her memory for
indicators why he had turned out like he had. Apollonia
regarded herself as level headed and a practical thinker.
She knew that, although she had never had the pleasure
of feeding a baby from her own breast, she still
possessed a maternal instinct. This instinct had kept her
nephew away from trouble for most of his childhood.
She was the one her sister depended on to intervene
when Damianos was in trouble at school; she was the
person who explained to him about right and wrong; she
was the person he came to in his early teenage years
when he was ostracised from a group of so called friends

A Lock up on Crete

and she was the one who paid for a child psychiatrist for him. It turned out that he had severe dyslexia which had led to frustration at school and beyond. God knows how his teachers hadn't picked up on it, she thought; he couldn't even pick up a simple book and read it. Her heart went out to him as she worked the cold winter streets to employ a private tutor to help with his dyslexia. However, within weeks, her sister felt it was unnecessary and finished the tuition, much to her dismay. Apollonia thought she had always been discreet as to how she earned extra income, soliciting just far away enough from her home town to avoid recognition. She had taken the bus to the port city of Sitia where there was an abundance of sailors to relieve and pamper. She doubted her sister was wise enough to figure it out though but all the same she had suddenly put a stop to Damianos' much needed tuition.

If only she had been able to stay in Iraepetra, maybe she could have tutored him herself - after all, she had been blessed with the brains of her family. Unfortunately, when she was forced to move from Iraepetra, her nephew's behaviour took a turn for the worse and his infatuation with the tourist girls resulted in his downfall.

She sighed to herself as she followed the familiar bus route, meandering through shuttered seaside villages and olive groves stripped bare of their fruit from the previous month's harvest. She had never been abroad or even taken a boat from the island but she knew Crete

A Lock up on Crete

was the best place on earth to live. She closed her eyes and braced herself for Iraepetra.

Once off the bus, Apollonia shielded her face with her black scarf and followed directions to the greenhouse that Damianos had relayed to her the night before on the telephone.

She could just make out the silhouettes of two people as she approached the last greenhouse in the row. Rita, the Dutch wife of Fotis also caught a glimpse of a black clad silhouette scuttling outside.

'Can I help you?' Rita asked as she blocked the way of the opening of the greenhouse.

'Yes, I would like to speak with Zoe,' she said in her politest voice. Rita wasn't convinced of her guise of a dear little lady who wouldn't harm a fly so imparted no information. She knew exactly who the witch was and was tempted to play her at her own game. Just then Zoe returned from the outside toilet, bumping into Apollonia.

'Zoe. I am Damianos's aunt. I come to ask you something please,' she said scooping up her black skirt that collected earth as it trailed on the ground.

'Yes, I know who you are. What do you want?'

'I understand you are both in a little bother so I can offer you my advice,' Apollonia explained, realising she was not orchestrating her plan very well as Rita towered above her, with no intention to move away.

'I think you should go now,' admonished Rita, waving her arm in the direction of the end of the row of greenhouses which led across to the beach.

A Lock up on Crete

'I also think you will find that I am not in trouble- just your nephew,' added Zoe feeling super confident with Rita beside her.

'I can offer you money if you don't press charges Zoe. You will like my offer. Think about it and let me know. Here is my number.'

Zoe and Rita escorted the wily black figure to the perimeter fence of the greenhouses. Apollonia turned right, sneaked a backward glance and made her way to the bus station.

Zoe and Damianos
Court hearing, Neapoli Law Courts

Zoe had enjoyed her week with Rita in the greenhouse. They had got along really well and it had been just the distraction she needed. She felt tired but refreshed at the same time from the manual work. Fotis had presented her with a brown envelope on her last afternoon and she was pleased when she tore it open on her return to the apartment that it was indeed a generous amount. She wondered if Rita had slipped a little extra, just in case she needed to pay court costs. Zoe hadn't readily told her about the factory incident. Rita had had a knack of subtle probing which had resulted in Zoe pouring her heart out to her. The amicable Dutch lady had been astounded by her story and vowed to help out in any way she possibly could. She was expecting her second child so Zoe assured her that she already had a lot of support and also had a good relationship with Tony the tourist policeman. It was actually a relief to find out from Rita that Tony was a genuine and revered policeman would not allow family connections hinder the support he was giving to Zoe.

Dressed in dark trousers and a white cotton jumper with her hair in a bun, Zoe braced herself for the day ahead. Theo insisted upon driving her to the Neapoli Law Courts where she was to attend at 2pm.

'Are you ready, Zoe?' Theo asked as she slid into the passenger seat of his comfortable Mercedes.

'Ready as I'll ever be Theo,' Zoe replied, pleased that she had slept well and after a bonding session with Tia and Mel the previous evening, felt a strange kind of calm. Rita had also popped by with her adorable little boy with his tight blonde curls and subtly passed her a pill. Zoe had decided not to take the pill, having promptly flushed it down the toilet.

Theo passed Zoe a bottle of water and informed her that the journey would take about an hour, dependent if the shepherds were moving their herds. They continued uphill taking the inland road rather than the coastal route.

'I have to drop off some olives in a village nearby. My brother sold his olive groves and now regrets it,' Theo announced as the bullet pitted sign welcomed them to Kritsa.

'No problemo Theo. Tell me, why do most of the roadside signs have bullet holes in them?' Zoe had been intrigued from the first time she had seen them scattering the countryside.

A Lock up on Crete

'Ahhh that is because here in Crete there is a local preoccupation with target practice and believe it or not, gun ownership is one of the highest in the world,' Theo explained to Zoe whose facial expression showed both concern and wonderment.

'Oh that's a bit scary Theo,' she added as he smiled.

'The amazing thing is Zoe, gun crime is virtually non-existent here in Crete. It is purely for those warrior type of males who find it their duty to be prepared for the enemy: after all we have been invaded many times in the past.'

'Interesting,' Zoe added as they approached the hilltop village and Theo turned the Merc down a narrow gravel path.

'Theo mou, Theo mou,' rejoiced a middle age woman. Zoe couldn't quite make out what was moving under her arm until she got closer and she realised it was a live chicken clucking in unison with every step she took towards her brother in law.

'Eleni, Eleni,' Theo embraced her as the chicken fell to the floor shedding some feathers along the way. Theo then hauled the two sacks of plump olives from the boot of his Merc as Eleni clapped her hands with joy. It was such a natural and genuine act of kindness Zoe thought as Theo carried the sacks into the small whitewashed cottage with the ubiquitous Greek blue shutters. After the loudest animated chat with his sister in law that Zoe had witnessed to date, they bid their farewells and continued on their journey to Neapoli.

A Lock up on Crete

They rode in relative silence as they took the road from Kritsa down to Agios Nikolaos where they stopped for some fuel and a cheese pie. Zoe looked at the time. They had about fifteen to twenty minutes left of their journey as the cheese pie started to irritate her stomach.

'Are you ok Zoe,' Theo asked as they neared Neapoli. Zoe nodded as Theo continued. 'Now when we arrive, Tony will take over and if anyone asks you anything either in Greek or English outside of the court rooms, do not answer. Try to focus on your composure and remember you are the innocent person. I will be in the gallery. Look for me. Focus your attention on me.'

'Thank you Theo.

Ten minutes later they were nearing the administrative town of Neapoli.

'Oh what's that building there Theo?' Zoe then realised what the imposing grey buildings surrounded with a barbed wire fence must be as they indicated to leave the national road.

'That is the second prison of Crete. The other is in Chania. Do not be surprised if Damianos is sent there today.'

Zoe's stomach churned over and over with sudden realisation that this may well be the outcome of the court case.

The Court of First Instance, Neapoli Law Courts

On first sight, the pretty pink and white façade of the law courts standing proud next to the large ornate church of the Blessed Virgin was not as intimidating as Zoe had imagined. Tony greeted them in the manicured

A Lock up on Crete

garden area and took over as they entered through an ornate iron door into a vestibule. There they waited until a guard opened a double wooden door standing aside to allow them inside .The sheer vastness of the court room made Zoe gasp.

'Zoe. Take a deep breath. It is a big room but focus on your breathing,' Tony instructed as he led her to their seat on the second level. She searched the sea of faces for any sign of Theo. Instead she saw Apollonia! Dressed in her usual black widow weeds even though she never married and had never been a widow, the gallery row dwarfed her as she sat on her own, scanning the room like a radar. Instinctively, Zoe averted her gaze and spotted Theo. She forced a smile as he reciprocated. The palms of her hands were wet with perspiration as Tony handed her a handkerchief.

An hour later, having endured countless criminal cases brought to the dock, she heard her name.

Zoe Matthews, Zoe Matthews.

Zoe's feet were rooted to the faded wooden floor as her name swirled around in her head. Tony took her by the shoulder and guided her to the wooden stand in the centre of the court room. He placed the weathered brown bible into her hand and read out her oath in Greek. Tony acted as her voice as he translated from Greek to English and vice versa. It was just as well, Zoe thought, as she couldn't imagine even a whisper of a sound coming out of her mouth right there in the voluminous, packed court room. There was so much commotion as other cases were being conducted at the same time - lawyers competing with each other; loud

A Lock up on Crete

voices criss- crossing one another; people exiting and entering at random times. Zoe tried to focus on what Tony was translating for her as he squeezed her hand. 'Sorry,' she squeaked as a lady produced a glass of water for her.

She downed the water in one, refocussing again to hear the judge call for

'Damianos Kazantakis, Damianos Kazantakis.' It amused her a little even at this serious time, how the Greeks always repeated a name or short phrase. However, this wasn't the time to lose focus she chided herself as Tony directed her to their seat and a smart looking Damianos rose in the dock opposite.

Zoe watched his facial expressions. He looked super confident in his black leather jacket. Zoe could hardly believe that he was actually wearing an item of clothing which could actually be used as evidence! Zoe had not pressed charges about the factory incident and she was also relieved that Costas and Vasilis had decided to drop the charge too: it could have done more harm than good and they had been informed by Tony that Zoe had been heavily advised to press charges on the Istanbul/passport, which would have more impact.

Damianos's smirk gradually morphed into a frown as Zoe's passport was passed around the judges for inspection. Zoe searched for Apollonia but could only see Theo as he stretched his legs in the confines of the tightly packed wooden benches. Tony nudged Zoe and she followed his eyes to where Apollonia stood at one of the witness desks in deep conversation. Damianos stood down from the dock where he was handcuffed and taken away. Apollonia let out a wail and tried to follow her nephew. Two female guards took her by her shoulder and directed her to a separate room.

'Zoe. Justice has been done,' Tony told her as they made their way outside and met up with Theo.

'What was the outcome Tony?' she asked feeling rather foolish by having to ask again.

'He is going to the cells and has a one year jail sentence unless he is bailed.'

Zoe's stomach churned at the prospect of her ex-boyfriend having to go to the prison a few hundred metres away overlooking the national road, which in the tourist season would be busy with vehicles and occupants having a wonderful holiday. Irony at its most mocking!

Could it have all been prevented she thought. There were so many emotions racing through her veins, she decided to say less rather than more and say the wrong thing.

'Thank you for being there for me Tony and Theo. Can we go back now?'

'Yes, yes, I have some more olives for my friend who lives near Hersonissos which is only a short distance from here if that is good with you,' Theo asked as Zoe chuckled and nodded.

They arrived back in Iraepetra in the early evening after being delayed at Theo's friend house who had insisted they had a tour of his new tourist gift shop. He had insisted Zoe choose a souvenir free of charge. She chose the blue evil eye – to ward away evil spirits – very apt, she had mused. When Theo mentioned Hersonnisos, Zoe envisaged the beachfront with the new bars and nightlife that were rapidly springing up, not a village up on the hill.

'Ahh Zoe, you see this village is Old Hersonnisos but is still regarded as the real Hersonnisos. The reason why it is not near the sea is that most of the coast of Crete was uninhabited except for a few fishing huts for the fishermen to stay overnight while fishing the sea. The village of the area was higher up to keep them safe from pirates and invaders. It is only with the tourist boom that the coast has become used,' Theo explained as they pulled into his friend's tight driveway.

'So are there any tourists that go up to the villages?'

'Yes, yes. They are becoming curious like you, wondering why the older generations did not live by the sea and that is why there are many new tavernas opening once again and tourist shops like what my friend owns. He doesn't regret the move from Iraepetra after also selling his greenhouses. I think he likes the nightlife down on the coast,' he winked.

'Yes I think some of my brother's friends have been on a package holiday round here. I think it was Malia,' Zoe added, wondering what it was like to go on a girl's holiday.

'Yes that would make sense as my friend said it was mainly British in Malia and mainly the Scandinavian in Hersonnisos. He tells me they are all crazy when they have had alcohol and there are plenty of sights around the towns after midnight. He says they turn from polite tourists during the day to crazy animals at night.'

'Yep, that's the northern European mentality. Not my cup of tea,' agreed Zoe.

'I like that expression Zoe. It makes me smile. I think here in Crete we would say *not our cup of Frappe.'*

News of the court hearing spread like wildfire. Damianos had spent a night in the court cell and spent the next day and subsequent days in Agios Nikolaos with his aunt. Apollonia had paid for his bail and had come over to Iraepetra to collect his belongings before swiftly taking a taxi back. Zoe wasn't surprised and would rather it have turned out like it did as after all, that prison, like prisons are meant to, looked absolutely horrendous. Zoe didn't feel many emotions - she was just glad that it was all over.

Chapter 20

Zoe spent the next few days with Rita at the greenhouses. She had an idea that Rita had told her husband that she needed extra help now she was nearly full term. There was very little to do now, except for weeding which suited Zoe; it reminded her of back home where her father made sure his children knew a flower from a weed in their manicured garden.

A Lock up on Crete

Rita, conscious not to wear herself out, suggested a quick break. She upturned two plastic crates and handed Zoe an iced cold frappe that she produced from the cool box.

'Zoe. I am working next week serving drinks at the big Bouzouki night here we have in the hotel up the road. Shall I ask if they need more staff? It could be fun for the night. Fotis doesn't really want me to work with only a few weeks to go but I could say I could take the orders and you could carry the drinks for me,' Rita's eyes sparkled as she held out her hand for Zoe to help her from her kneeling position among the weeds. 'Even if there isn't a job, I will pay you half of my wages. It is good for me to get out of the house every now and again to be honest; there's only so much crochet I can endure with Fotis's mama and yiayia.' Rita raised her eyes to the plastic ceiling of the greenhouse and mimicked how she crotched sat on the low plastic crate.

'That sounds like fun Rita. Yes please ask. I am actually wondering what to do myself after the court hearing. I feel like I have caused grief here in Iraepetra for some people and would like to move on, possibly go to Israel or maybe go home and recharge my batteries,' Zoe confessed. Although she could talk like this to Tia and Mel, it was also good to speak with Rita too. As if reading her thoughts, Rita asked,

'So how about your two friends. What are they going to do?'

'I'm not really sure. I guess I have been too involved in my own problems to ask how they are and what they want to do in the near future. I know Mel likes her job baking and is quite keen on an ex pat who lives in Elounda. Tia is with her Greek boyfriend most of the time now and she likes working for his sister at the salon and is learning Greek. So who knows?' Zoe explained as she shrugged her shoulders.

'Your friend. Is she with Andreas? She looks like a Greek girl I think?'

'Yes that's Tia.They met on the second night we arrived in Iraepetra,' expalined Zoe as she tipped the wheelbarrow full of weeds outside.

'Ahh, I hear rumours that he may be inheriting his uncle's kafenion. I hear also that the wicked witch Apollonia is contesting the will,' Rita revealed.

'Wow you know more than I do! I wonder if Tia has told me and I've been too wrapped up in my own stuff to listen. Oh I feel awful now.' Zoe reached for two bottles of water and handed one to Rita.

'It's funny how you call Apollonia the wicked witch as that is what we named her after she accused us of giving Manolis Mariakis a fake note,' Tia remarked.

'You are joking! Five years ago when I first came to Iraepetra as a touristee - that is exactly what she accused me of. I had taken my clothes to the launderette and she insisted I paid with a 2,000 drachma note but it was definitely a 5,000 note.' Both women shook their heads in unison as they shut the door of the green house for the day and Zoe tipped the weeds in the large compost pile.

With Damianos in Agios Nikolaos, Zoe felt a sense of relief and calm. She still popped into Michalis's souvlaki stall to check that he was well and his take away gyros were still ten out of ten. Nothing was mentioned about the court case and Damianos and it reassured Zoe that she was still welcomed in Iraepetra. The following week she helped Rita at the bouzouki night. It turned out to be just the tonic she needed as it developed into quite a slap stick evening with a twist of the bizarre.

'Ooopa, ooopa.' Zoe joined in with the dancers as she periodically swept the dance floor piled up with smashed plates. She had heard about the plate smashing and realised how cathartic and fun it was. The guests bought the special plates at the reception to smash over each other as they danced to the live music. It was hilarious - especially when Zoe broke the handle of the broom in half clearing up the mountain of plates in the middle of the dance floor. There were plenty of hoots of laughter as she continued hunched over a half sized broom and swept the stack of broken plates into the corridor. Rita then asked her to take the empty glasses into the enormous kitchen to put into the dishwasher. Rita had been sneaking whisky and cokes to Zoe and by the third or fourth they had taken effect. So, when the whole of the glass window imploded into the kitchen, Zoe thought that she was seeing things caused by the inebriated state she was in. She stood there looking onto the floor, carpeted with broken glass in utter disbelief. Rita came in to see where she was and gasped.
'Jeez Zoe. What have you done?'

'Nothing I just emptied the dishwasher and I heard a bang then turned round and this happened,' she explained, suddenly sober.

'Jeez, it could have killed you! Here, let me check you for glass,' Rita urged as she spun her round and inspected her shoes for any glass shards.

'What do you think has shattered the window?' Zoe asked a bewildered Rita as she sat on the cold metal worktop. Like a bull ready for the ring, the hefty bouzouki manager marched in. it was difficult even for Rita to convince him that the whole of the window had just shattered of its own accord. He marched over to the 6ft squared window with a gaping hole in it which looked into a lemon grove. It was a mystery how it had happened, with no evidence of any projectile having been thrown at it. The manager spoke in halted Greek to Rita. The only word Zoe could decipher was *chrimata* – money!

It was midnight as the last of the bouzouki guests dispersed into the cool night air to take their taxis back home. Thankfully, Rita was handed the full amount of money for the night's work despite the shattered window and shared it with Zoe. The slight hiccup with the phantom window smasher was not mentioned as they got into Rita's car. Once inside, both women roared with laughter at the sheer craziness of the events of the night.

The next morning Zoe woke with a whiskey induced hangover. Tia or Mel had dutifully placed a glass of water

A Lock up on Crete

and painkillers on the bedside table. It suddenly dawned on her that the three of them were so involved in their own bubble lives in Iraepetra that they had lost real touch with each other: Apart from when they returned from work in the evening they hadn't had real fun and gotten really drunk together for ages.

Feeling as though she had burnt herself out, Zoe confided in Rita that she had decided to return home in time for her 21st birthday. Although she would have liked to celebrate in sunny Crete, family beckoned. By the afternoon, Zoe had decided to tell Tia and Mel her intentions in the hope they would understand. She would also give a week notice so they could sort out a cheaper room for the two of them.

'Oh Zoe. Of course we understand. In fact I am thinking of moving to Elounda to see how the summer season reacts to my tarts. Bill says I can stay with him and I do love it there. There's a certain magnetism about it and I can't wait to take the trip over to Spinalonga which just for your information is named after me, Miss Melissa Longthorn.'

'Bill the magnet, more like,' Tia teased as she gave each girl a hug.

'I have news too,' she said with a huge grin on her face.

'Oh my God. Are You?' screeched Zoe as she rubbed Tia's tummy.

'No! Of course not,' Tia held out her finger to reveal a sweet little engagement ring. Zoe pulled out the whiskey bottle that Rita must have accidently placed in her bag at the end of their shift and filled three small glasses.

A Lock up on Crete

'Here's to new beginnings and amazing memories,' the three girls chimed as they hugged and passed round the box of tissues.

PART 2   - 31 years later

Chapter 1

Tia and Andreas, Iraepetra, Crete February 2015

Andreas had just finished the accounts for the Snak Stop. He was relieved he didn't have to make the daily two hour return journey from Agios Nikolaos to Iraepetra anymore. Since his accident he was more than content to sit on his balcony, a mere fifty metres from the sea, mending watches and the occasional pieces of jewellery. Tia had just returned from Agios Nikolaos, a journey she made each Friday to pay the wages to the staff. He always made sure he had ordered their favourite souvlaki delivery and as always, right on time, Michalis delivered it to his door personally. Both men would enjoy a few shots of local Raki before Tia arrived home and Michalis returned to work. Life was now predictable and comfortable and was just what the doctor had ordered for a healthy recovery.

Mel and Tommy Little   New Zealand 2015

A Lock up on Crete

Home had not been the answer to her heartache when her relationship with Bill in Elounda slowly burned out just like her bakewell tarts had. Fortunately, Mel looked forward and never backwards. Thus, she said goodbye to her folks back home, jumped on a plane to Tel Aviv and caught the Kibbutz bug. She met Tommy Little, a fellow Lancastrian, while working in the orange juice factory. Their eyes had met over the conveyer belt as they scanned for rotten oranges. For a whole year they travelled the length and breadth of Israel, working on the Kibbutz's along the way. Eventually, they returned to Lancaster in an effort to put down some roots. Unfortunately, their attempt was futile and not being able to settle, they decided to emigrate to the other side of the world. New Zealand proved to be just their cup of tea and a slice of cake. With a population of 1 human to 3 sheep it was about the same size of the UK with familiar countryside but without the traffic jams, crime rate and population density. Mel still loved to bake and ran a successful online business. Tommy was also able to work from home. With their menagerie of pets they were quite content and relished in the thought that they had plenty of options between them. Apart from her parents and family, Mel missed two other special people – Tia and Zoe. Would she ever see them again she often wondered as she gazed out of her window looking over the Palliser Bay, a view she would never tire of.

Zoe and her mother, Elounda Crete 2015
Zoe and her mother Eve, had read the book 'The Island' and discussed it in detail with each other on numerous

A Lock up on Crete

occasions while having afternoon tea in their local tea rooms. It was 2015 and it just so happened that they were both celebrating milestone birthdays.

'Zoe I really would like us both to go away for our special birthdays this year,' Eve relayed over the phone one dull August day.

'You mean just us two without any children or husbands in tow?'

'Yes I think so if you could arrange it. You know where I would love to go Zoe?' Eve didn't wait for her daughter to answer. 'I'd love to go to Crete and visit the island of Spinalonga, you know the one we read about in The Island.' Zoe could envisage her mum waiting for her reply with everything crossed including making the sign of the cross.

'Brilliant idea mum. Oh to be back in Crete again. We could try and find Tia and Andreas too.' Zoe's voice was a decibel higher as she imagined the scene.

'Leave it with me Zoe. I'm thinking the end of the season as I don't like it too hot.'

Zoe could hardly contain her excitement as she punched the air in her kitchen and treated herself to a coffee from her new pod machine. Crete! She was going back to her beloved Crete after what, thirty years?

Heraklion, Crete

Heraklion airport, in slight need of an uplift welcomed mother and daughter to its island as they breathed in the warm evening air. They found the public bus hiding amongst the tourist coaches and paid the small fare.

A Lock up on Crete

An hour later they stepped down from the bus and were directed over to their modest hotel, where they were welcomed by the barman. Without any deliberation they ordered a cocktail each and allowed the niggles of everyday life back in England wash away as they sat in some comfy bucket chairs. Eve broke the comfortable silence.

'So do you think we will be able to track Tia down Zoe? I can't believe you haven't kept in touch all these years to be truthful?'

'Well we could get the bus to Iraepetra but it will take a whole day if you're up for it,'

'Yeah course I am. I'm intrigued to find her and her husband,' replied Eve as she ordered two more Mojitos and a packet of crisps.

Zoe had never relayed the story about the trouble with Damianos and the passport to her mother all those years ago. She just hoped that they would be able to find Tia and Andreas and by a stroke of genius they would actually be home. Zoe had been in touch with Mel on Facebook and after the initial awkwardness on both parts, feeling slightly guilty that either had kept in contact after Crete, they both reasoned that thirty years ago, apart from traditional snail mail they hadn't had the convenience of modern technology – no mobile phones, no computers and no social media. With Face book messenger and Google earth, Zoe had been able to see where Mel lived in New Zealand with Tommy Little. Fortunatley, Mel was under her maiden name on Facebook. Zoe couldn't quite imagine addressing her friend as Mel Little, although it did have a quirky ring to it. She could just make out, as she zoomed in on Google Earth, that they had a decent size plot and no doubt had built their self- sufficient lifestyle on it. It looked idyllic and she was so happy that she had found true love. It was just a shame she was on the other side of the world. Thus, Zoe was prepared to take a chance and travel with her mother to Iraepetra. She would ask around the bars and tavernas on the seafront for the whereabouts of Tia and Andreas; she couldn't envisage them moving away somehow.

Before the trip they needed to take the trip that had spurred them to come to Crete in the first place – the long awaited trip to the former leper colony of Spinalonga, that Mel had enthused about long before the novel 'The Island' was written.

The water was choppy as they neared the shores of Spinalonga and the allure of the island evoked memories of reading the book. Zoe and her mother sat in silence with lumps in their throats as the imposing stone buildings started to take shape the nearer they approached. They had decided to take the short ferry from the tiny pier in the village of Plaka just like the poor lepers would have done up until the 1950's. The difference was that Zoe and her mother would be able to return to Plaka unlike the lepers that had been sent over, never to return to their loved ones again. The short distance from Plaka to their adopted home of Spinalonga could have been a million miles away - distance made no difference to their fate. They were there until death took them.

A Lock up on Crete

There were only a few dry faces as the small boat docked at the island. Zoe and Eve paid the entrance fee and took the tunnel through to the cobbled streets of the former leper colony. Apart from the few tour guides milling about, time could have stopped still as they walked down the main street passing what would have been the leper's houses and shops. In fact it could have also been reminiscent of any other Cretan village of abandoned houses that were not too far away on the mainland. Wooden doors creaked on their hinges as Eve looked through a small hole which led her eyes into a large open space.

'Zoe, come here. I wonder why this room is so big.' Zoe was already reading the plaque.

'Oh Mum, come here where we can see it better,' she guided her mother down to the steps.

'Oh God! This large room is the quarantine area where the new patients were hosed down to clean them from infections and such like. Oh and you remember in the book there was mention of Dante's gate?'

'Is that it then?' Eve asked her daughter as they joined tourists taking selfies on the jetty.

'I do think it's a bit inappropriate all this selfie taking,' Eve said as Zoe pointed to the large opening in the old fortress wall which led into a long low tunnel known as Dante's gate.

'Here let's read this plaque about it,' Zoe said as a group of tourists laughed and joked much to Eve's chagrin.

There are two entrances to Spinalonga, one being the lepers entrance, a tunnel known as Dante's Gate. This was probably taken from Dante's inferno and his

A Lock up on Crete

description of the gate to hell. This was so named because the patients felt trepidation as to what would happen to them once they had arrived on the island. However, it was the in their best interest to be sent here as once on the island they received food, water, medical attention and social security payments. These amenities had been unavailable to Crete's leprosy patients, as they mostly lived in the area's caves, away from civilisation.

Eve and her daughter soaked in the humbling atmosphere of the fortress island as they walked the perimeter and passed small churches and the graveyard, reminding each other about the extracts from the famous novel. Time had unfortunately rushed by as they waited in the throng of visitors, desperately searching for their return boats. They looked deranged as though if they missed their return boat they would be marooned and transported back in time and become lepers themselves.

'There's nowt as queer as folk,' both women agreed as they waited patiently for the smallest boat to take them back to Plaka, reminding themselves to return when it was out of season where they could stay longer than the allocated hour and a half.

With Spinalonga ticked off their 'to do list' and after a restful day lapping up the last hot rays of the October sun their next quest was the search for Tia and Andreas. The next morning they took the bus from the stop in the tiny centre of Elounda and changed at Agios Nikolaos. On the next bus to Iraepetra they passed sleepy small

A Lock up on Crete

holiday resorts, in the process of closing for the season to start vital renovations. Eve marvelled at the Bay of Mirabello and behind her sunglasses, stared at the locals getting on and off the bus. She was a great people watcher and was in her element. Zoe smiled as her mother nudged her as a little Yiayia in her black widow weeds shuffled down the narrow aisle of the bus. Eve couldn't help but notice the old ladies feet. Yia yia, bless her, was wearing odd flip flops.

After an interesting journey, they arrived at the bus terminus of Iraepetra, which thirty one years ago, Zoe had arrived fresh faced with Tia and Mel. It hadn't changed one little bit – even the laundrette was still there next door – she imagined what she would do if she saw the wicked witch Apollonia as she dismissed the shadow of a stooped black clad figure shuffling inside – surely the witch had long since passed.

Zoe turned round to see where her mother had got to – she was helping the little Yiayia off the steep steps from the bus. Eve said goodbye to the Yiayia as Zoe found her bearings and directed them to Fotis's café bar on the seafront.

They sat down in the same spot Zoe had done in 1984 when Damianos had purposely rolled a coin her way.

'Oh! Look Zoe, it's named after you,' Eve exclaimed.

Zoe looked up at the updated sign overhead and gasped slightly.

Café bar Zoi

'Well I wouldn't go that far Mum. I wasn't that popular! Zoi means life in Greek, so I guess translated, it says Café bar Life.' Zoe watched her mother as she soaked

A Lock up on Crete

everything up around her like a natural Greek sponge; it was like an explosion to her senses.

'You love it don't you Mum.'

'I do! I knew it was a good idea to come to Crete for both of us – I love it here.'

Both women sighed at the same time then burst out in laughter just as the waiter came to take their order.

'Theloume thia bira parakalo,' Zoe said in Greek to the young waiter.

'Oh. Zoe. Have you just ordered two beers in Greek?'

'Sure have Mother,' Zoe replied.

'I just hope we can find Tia, Zoe. Hey why don't you ask him?' Eve suggested as the young waiter set two beers down on the table.

'No he's far too young. I will take us to the restaurant Mel used to work at and ask there. I hope you are hungry?'

Warm memories flooded back as they walked the short distance on the seafront to Medusa's. Zoe was pleased to see that apart from a few more trendy bars, time had stood still in this important agricultural town. The sea still made its presence known as it battered the short sea wall, splashing onto the seafront promenade. Each establishment they passed evoked different memories for Zoe as they came across the sign for Medusa's restaurant. Zoe gazed up at the sign. Although the sea had ravaged and rusted the edges, it looked to be the same sign as the faded snakes wriggled from the head of the notorious gorgon, Medusa.

A Lock up on Crete

Surely Mr M would have long since gave up work, Zoe thought as they entered the darkened interior. A young girl worked furiously kneading dough and making fresh pita bread. A middle aged man with jet black hair and similar moustache cleaned the bar area while an older man with thick white hair sat at a table with a cigarette dangling from his mouth, tallying up some bills. Zoe took a deep breath and walked up to where he sat.

'Excuse me. Could I ask how long you have worked here please?' it wasn't the question Zoe was thinking of but it had just came out more in keeping with the Greek way of direct questioning rather than the English way. It really didn't matter anyway as the man looked up with a frown.

'Too long!' he replied, motioning for Zoe and Eve to sit down.

'Katsi katsi, sit sit,' he ordered while he shuffled his bills into a pack and bound them with a rubber band.

'I think you may remember my friend then who worked here in 1984, Mel.'

'Meli! Yes red hair Meli. Was you here at the same time?' he asked, shouting an order to the young man at the bar.

'Let me introduce myself. I am Eros and I was Meli's boss. Oh I can still remember the smell of her baking. Tell me. How is she? Is she here?' Eros's eyes suddenly lit up as he looked beyond the interior, wondering if she would suddenly appear from nowhere.

'Pleased to meet you again, Eros. Mel never mentioned your name. She called you Mr M! It's a beautiful name by the way. Oh sorry, afti ine mitera mou – this is my mother.'

Eros suddenly took to his feet and held out his hand to Eve, leaving a small kiss upon her hand.

'Meli is she here?' Eros repeated as he motioned for the young barman to come over with the cocktail menu.

'No sorry Eros unfortunately she isn't. Mel lives in New Zealand now. I was wondering if you knew where I could find my other friend Tia,' Zoe said with a little crackle in her voice.

'Tia. Ahh, she married Andreas,' You are here to visit them?'

'Yes but I don't know where to find them. I lost touch and I haven't seen them for thirty one years.'

'Trianda ena? Thirty one? Po Po Po. Long time. I think I remember you now. You and Damianos Kazantakis?' Eros twiddled with his moustache as he began to piece the connections together. Zoe became a little impatient pulling at her bobbed hair like she had always done when things are not just going quite the way she envisaged.

'Stop pulling your hair Zoe. It looks weird,' whispered her mum with the cocktail menu between them.

'Yes that's right. So do you know where I can find them? Do they still live here?

'Yes, yes. I am phoning now.' Zoe's heart pounded in her chest as Eros spoke into his phone.

'Oh he is not answering. Maybe he is out. He does not have a mobile phone. So come, I show you where they live.'

A Lock up on Crete

Eve was amazed as they climbed into Eros's car and he drove them a little further towards the beach where Zoe and the girls had, thirty one years ago lived in the same apartment. After pointing it out to her mother to where she once lived, Eros pulled up a few hundred yards away at a modest apartment block. He promptly pipped his horn a few times before getting out of his car and shouting at the top of his voice directed at the closed door on the third floor balcony.

'Andreas, Tia, Andreas, Tia,' he bellowed.

Eventually a tall figure appeared on the balcony, peering down to see what the commotion was. Eros spoke in Greek as Andreas almost dangled off the balcony for a closer look.

'Zoe, Zoe! Tia, Tia ella ella,' Tia appeared on the balcony and after a quick explanation she yelled Zoe's name over and over again. Realising that they couldn't carry on much longer yelling each other's name, Tia fled down the stairs and rushed into Zoe's outstretched arms.

'Mel, Mel! ,' she called to Eve after they finally released each other.

'No Tia. This is my mum, you remember? Mel lives in New Zealand now.'

'Oh, sorry! I got a bit mixed up. My brain feels like it's going to explode! Of course I remember you Mrs Matthews. It's been three decades and you honestly have not changed one little bit! That's why I thought you were Mel! Come on let's go up to the apartment to Andreas,' Tia urged as Eve hung back a little and thanked Eros.

A Lock up on Crete

The staircase up to her apartment were the most dangerous ones Zoe had ever encountered rising up in a spiral without a handrail in site. Zoe and her mum were relieved to have made it to the door where an older but still good looking Andreas stood. Zoe couldn't help but notice his pronounced limp as he turned to go inside his modest apartment, moving stuff out of the way with his wooden crutch.

'Zoe, Zoe. Why you took so long to come back?' Andreas questioned as he motioned for the women to go through to the balcony.

'I know, I know. It's been thirty one years but now I am here it seems like only yesterday. Oh it is just amazing to see you both. I'm so glad we found you. Andreas switched his attention from Zoe to Eve. The slight confusion etched in his eyes gave a hint of his reluctance to ask if the smart older lady was Zoe's mother or maybe her sister. Zoe put him out of his confusion.

'Andreas, please meet my mother Eve.' Without allowing Andreas to react she carried on.

'Oh Why aren't you on Facebook?' she asked Tia as she accepted the extra cold Mythos beer with the pull off top that her long lost friend had produced from the fridge.

'Oh long, long story Zoe. Tia will tell you later,' said Andreas as he took a gulp of beer and revealed to Eve that he honestly thought she was Zoe's sister. He excused himself and returned with a plastic 2 litre bottle of clear liquid.

A Lock up on Crete

'This is my family's home produced Raki. The best in Iraepetra!' Eve wondered if it was akin to a Women's Institute competition for the best Victoria sponge. 'To us! Yammas!' all four cheered as they raised their glasses and downed the neat raki.

'Oh my Lord! Wow! What is that?' Eve visibly shook as the clear liquid passed through her throat and burned into her stomach.

'Here soak it up with this, Mrs Matthews.' Tia had whipped up a selection of meze dishes in a matter of seconds from her plentiful kitchen. There were small plates of black misshapen olives, chunks of bread, creamy feta cheese and fresh cherries. Eve helped herself to the delicious saucer like plates, savouring each bite.

'Please call me Eve, Tia. I remember when the three of you set off from my house to come to Crete with your backpacks on and adventure in your eyes. I was envious. I wanted to turn back the clock and go with you,' Eve revealed as she took Tia's hand in hers.

'Actually Mum. Mel and I had backpacks. Madam here had a pull along suitcase with her stilettoes on when we arrived in Agios Nikolaos. Mel had to swap with Tia and lug it everywhere.'

'And look at you now agape mou,' Andreas jested as Tia looked down at her shorts, baggy t-shirt and flip flops.

'I think you'd better look at yourself too agape mou,' Tia retorted, winking at Zoe and Eve.

'Hey, we didn't warn you we were coming so you both don't look too bad considering it was a surprise,' Zoe chipped in as Eve nodded in agreement.

A Lock up on Crete

Tia walked by her husband to get some more beer from the fridge as he patted her behind affectionately. Zoe was pleased they were still besotted with each other after all this time.

'Ha, you know I say to Tia. I say, well Tia, you know you have had the best of me so now you have to take the rest of me,' joked Andreas as he pointed to his leg.

'Zoe, I show you my leg,' Andreas insisted as he rolled up his trouser leg.

'Ouch that looks like a shark bite!' exclaimed Zoe as her mother looked over the balcony to the sea averting her gaze from the deep scar on his thigh.

Tia nudged her husband to reprimand him as she returned with more beer, a plate of plump almonds and a heavy ornate photo album which she placed on the table. Andreas promptly replaced his trouser leg as Tia nodded her approval. Andreas sensed the interest in Zoe's body language so carried on.

'You know it was a stupid kamaki boy who did this to my leg! From bloody Athens he was. Showing off on his motorbike to his girlfriend and look what he left me with.' Andreas was clearly reliving the moment as Tia relayed the accident in his pickup truck that had happened four years ago, knowing how cathartic it was for her husband to get it off his chest now and again.

'The young malaca on the motorbike tried to overtake in a notorious tunnel just outside of Agios Nikolaos,' Tia continued as Andreas leant forward as if to warn them that it was his turn to speak.

'Two bloody years it took for the trial to go through. I know how you must have felt in that bloody court room in Neapoli Zoe.' Tia threw her husband a look as his mouth clamped shut. Tia hoped that Eve hadn't heard too much about her daughter's past problems in Iraepetra. Then again, Tia thought, Zoe may have already told her mother, hence the impromptu visit..

Zoe sensed an oncoming awkward moment if her mother had picked up on the mention of a court as she picked up the wedding album from the table.
'Ahhh the wedding album. At last I get to see it,' Zoe announced as Andreas excused himself to have a cigarette inside. Zoe passed it to her mother, giving her the honour of turning over the thick pages adorned with elaborate photos of Tia and Andreas' wedding day.
'Oh Tia, I just wish I could have come over for your wedding. I was stuck on the kibbutz in Israel amidst the Libyan Air Strikes and we weren't allowed to travel for fear that the nutcase Gaddafi struck Israel. Mel was in the same predicament as she was on a similar kibbutz at the same time. We did contemplate sneaking out or making a plausible excuse to leave but the restrictions on travel was limited. Mel and I were only an hour away from each other but could only speak on the phone. And that's the last I heard of her until the invention of Face book.'
After her third beer and second Raki, Tia couldn't hold back her tears any longer.
'Oh Zoe, I just can't believe you are actually here after all this time. I have often thought about you and what you were up to; if you ever married; if you had children.'

A Lock up on Crete

Zoe nodded and wondered whether to broach the subject of children to her. The tears were infectious as Eve welled up and the three of them openly allowed their tears to flow in the comfort of Tia and Andreas's home.

'I feel exactly the same Tia. It really is so good to see you both,' Zoe said turning to Andreas who had taken a back seat halfway in the apartment and halfway on the balcony.

'It is a big surprise Zoe. You always did surprises well,' he teased.

'What happened to Damianos?' Zoe asked as her mother excused herself to go to the toilet.

'Po po po. The last time we heard he was in Holland and that was shortly after you left and that is the last time anyone saw him unless his family know otherwise,' Andreas explained shrugging his shoulders and turning down his mouth as the Greeks do.

'Oh wow. I really did make an impact then hey?' All of a sudden Tia let out a tight squeak as her hand flew to her mouth and she rushed into the apartment.

'Oh my God, what's wrong?' Zoe looked at Andreas for any clarification.

'Andreas, Andreas. How can I have not remembered? It was Zoe's. Get it out of the safe,' Tia almost screamed at her husband as he rose from his chair and joined his wife in the small area of the lounge where he did his repairs. Zoe stared at the wall and focussed on a photo of a younger Tia and Andreas outside the Medusa restaurant hanging crooked on the wall.

A Lock up on Crete

Eve returned to join them as Andreas handed a small box to Tia as she laid it on some cloth on the balcony table.

'My locket!' It was Zoe's turn to be astonished as her hands flew to her mouth to stifle a scream. Tia and Andreas hugged each other as they watched the momentous revelation unfold.

'But, but, what's it doing here?' Zoe fumbled with her words as her mother stared in disbelief, lost for words, having recognised the locket.

'I knew it! I knew I had seen it somewhere before but I couldn't quite grasp where,' Tia recalled as they all huddled around the locket as if it was an ancient artefact.

'I thought I had misplaced it at the apartment and with everything that was going on at the time I didn't carry on the search for it. Besides I have a bad reputation of losing sentimental jewellery. My mum gave me this for my 18th birthday didn't you?' Eve nodded and smiled. 'I have always dreaded the question of its whereabouts you know Mum,' Eve placed her hand over her mouth as if to stifle a yelp. 'I even tried to find a replica to buy but nothing came close.'

'Well it is old. It was a birthday present from my friends for my 21st. And now finally it is reunited with us after thirty one years, thanks to you two,' Eve, the original owner of the locket placed, took it from Tia and carefully placed it into her daughter's palm.

'Now be more careful with it young lady,' Eve urged, shaking her head in both disbelief and contentment. She had often wondered why her daughter never seemed to

A Lock up on Crete

wear the locket but never thought too much into it. There was a comfortable silence while Andreas replenished their drinks. Tia held on to Zoe's arm as if to protect her friend and the locket while they allowed Andreas to continue the story.

'So, this is how the locket came to be in our possession. A few years ago, maybe five,' he said looking at Tia for confirmation. 'Apollonia, who is still alive, Zoe!' Andreas pre-emptied Zoe's reaction as she gasped. Tia picked up from her husband.
'So, we assumed Apollonia posted the locket through our letterbox one morning as Andreas was up here on the balcony having his morning cigarette and coffee. He thought he had seen an older Yia yia in black weeds, which there are many anyway. But he seemed to recall she had quickly looked up to the balcony before scuttling away. You remember her features Zoe?' 'Those beady black eyes and hooked nose,' Tia puffed as her eyes looked up to the sky. 'A real witch if ever I saw one!' she couldn't help but add. 'Well, Andreas didn't think much of it and then a few days later we found the envelope containing your locket wedged in a corner of the hall downstairs. There was just a note inside, asking for it to be repaired and that a young woman called Mary Elena would pick it up in a few weeks. A few months went by and still no one came so we looked at the envelope again for any clues and it looked like the previous address was still partly visible, so we tried to work it out. We could just about decipher two words – plyntirio and pasifais.

A Lock up on Crete

'Which mean what?' Zoe asked as Andreas apologised for not translating.

'plyntirio is Greek for launderette and pasifais is the word that stumped us. The only pasifias I knew was the name of a road in Agios Nikolaos near the jetty,' Andreas explained as Tia took over again.

'Now I know what you may be wondering -why didn't we investigate further? But if truth be told, we didn't want it to be returned to the wrong person and so we have kept it safe all these years. We did have a lot on at the time too with the Will and everything else but I'll continue later with that.'

'Tia recognised the locket from somewhere when I was fixing the clasp and so we opened it up but couldn't recognise the fading photographs in it. Here let me show you,' Andreas carefully opened the locket to reveal two photos either side.

'We asked nearly everyone in town if they recognised the babies but to no avail and to be fair it is hard to distinguish babies at that age.' All three nodded in agreement with Andreas as Zoe took the locket from her mother's slightly shaky hand.

'They might still be here,' Zoe said softly to her mother. 'Do you have a pin or needle please Tia?' Andreas reached over to his little workstation and handed Zoe a pin. They held their breath as Zoe carefully pulled the baby photos away with the pin and placed them on the table. Behind the photos lay black and white photos of a young woman and man.

'That's my mother and that's my father,' Zoe revealed as her fingers shook. She handed the locket to her mother.

A Lock up on Crete

'Yes that's us,' Eve gasped as she clutched the locket to her heart. 'If only your father was here to see it.' Eve's eyes glazed over as she was transported back to the past.

'Please Eve, can I take the locket?' Andreas asked holding out his palm. Eve hesitated a little until coming to her senses.

'Oh yes, sorry of course.'

'I need to clean it for you. It has lost its shine after all these years.' Andreas took a special cloth and carefully closed it and rubbed the outer gold until the sparkle returned.

'But who could the babies be in the photos?' Zoe asked. 'I was just thinking the same,' Eve said as Tia explained that no one in Iraepetra had recognised them all those years ago.

I'm so glad we kept it rather than chasing up to see if it was Apollonia who had dropped it off that morning,' Tia admitted as she addressed her husband. Andreas nodded and motioned her to carry on. 'And although we knew Apollonia worked in the launderette we both said if it was hers then she would have sent someone to collect. But after the business with the Will, the last person we wanted to help was Apollonia,' Tia could tell Zoe was eager to know the outcome of the Will. 'Zoe we will get to the Will soon but what I can't understand is how Apollonia had your locket and who the babies are because Apollonia never married and as far as we know didn't have any children?'

A Lock up on Crete

'That's a mystery to me too to be honest. I thought I had just misplaced it either at our apartment or when I was convalescing at Katerinas, Damianos's kindly aunt,' Zoe added, looking towards the choppy sea, which was becoming angrier with each hour that passed.

Zoe waited for her mother to go to the toilet again before she continued.

'Listen my mum doesn't know the story so we will have to be quick,' Zoe urged as she carried on. 'Damianos might have found it at Katerinas and gave it to Apollonia to take care of?'

'Or he gave it to Apollonia in return for some debt he had with her?' Andreas suggested as he rubbed his chin stubble.

'Hang on! What was the outcome of the court case Zoe?' Tia asked.

'His aunt bailed him out and I assumed at the time it was his aunt Katerina. Do you think it could have been his aunt Apollonia?' Zoe looked from Tia to Andreas like a tennis spectator. 'It makes more sense. At the time she was also contesting my uncle's will thinking she would inherit plenty of money. But then she didn't so maybe Damianos had to pay her back and he gave her your locket to pay his debt to her?' Andreas added as he moved his wooden crutch to stand up with.

'Oh wow, yes and that's the connection! Zoe, remember when I came to visit you at Katerina's when you had returned from Istanbul?' Tia asked as Zoe nodded.

'That's where I saw your locket! I used the toilet and it was hanging over the glass with your toothbrush in it and I was just about to advise you to move it somewhere safer when Katerina interrupted my thoughts and came into your room saying it was time for me to go!'

Tia helped her husband and placed the crutch under his arm as he excused himself.

'Hang on with the conversation until I come back from the toilet,' Andreas urged as he passed Eve in the darkened lounge.

'I wonder why this Apollo woman never collected it?' Eve mulled as she took her seat. 'Especially as she is still alive,' Zoe added, realising the need to continue talking about the locket rather than her fateful relationship with Damianos.

'She must have forgot or knew we wouldn't believe it was hers maybe,' Tia suggested as she fastened the locket over Zoe's neck.

'Well that sounds about right. So now we have sorted the mystery of the locket out it is now time for me to hear all about the Will,' Zoe suggested as she absently stroked the locket which had finally found its owner.

The story of the will of Andreas's uncle Manolis Mariakis

'O po po po, Zoe, Zoe. Where do we begin? It took two years to sort my uncle's will. We also had to go to the Law Courts in Neapoli and contest Apollonia's contesting of the will.

I will hand you over to Tia as she can explain better the English words. I will order food,' Andreas reached for the telephone as Tia shuffled in her chair and brought it closer to the table. Unconsciously, Zoe and Eve replicated her action.

'Andreas, before we get started can I ask what O po po po translates to in English? I never did find out.' Zoe asked.

'Ahh it is just like you say – oh my God –or you must be joking.'

'One more thing please. *Ime olos aftia,*' the limited Greek phrases Zoe knew came flooding back to her as she threw a little light on the next subject of the will.

'Ahh Zoe you remember a little of your Greek! Bravo,' Andreas said as he rose to go into the apartment to use the telephone.

'What did you say?' asked Eve.

'Sorry Mum. It means – I am all ears. Believe me, I didn't really pick up as much Greek as I should have done in the six months I was here. You see the younger generation, I mean in 1984 which included Andreas's age, were taught English at an early age in primary school. Eve listened eagerly as yet another revelation began to unfold.

As Andreas ordered the food, Tia took the opportunity to show Zoe and Eve her wedding album. Turning the pages carefully, the three women ooh'd and ahh'd at the beauty of Tia and her extremely handsome groom.

'Where is the church you were married in Tia?' asked Eve.

'Literally just up from here. You will have passed it from the bus station.'

'I wish I could have made your wedding Tia. I was gutted,' Zoe reflected.

'Ahhh it took a long time to sort out the wedding bans in the UK and then here. There was so much red tape at one point we nearly gave up on it but thought that living in sin wouldn't go down in this town,' Tia said as she lovingly placed the album back on the shelf.

Disturbing their thoughts, a young voice shouted up from below as Andreas lowered a plastic crate from the balcony. Tia broke into a smile as Zoe and her mum watched in awe as the delivery boy placed the take away food order in the crate and Andreas lifted it back up with the blue frayed rope.

'Oh wow. I've seen it all now!' That's a bit different from our Domino's pizza delivery back home!

Andreas placed the three boxes on the table as they devoured the fresh pizza washed down with a beer each.

'So where were we? Ahh yes, the bloody Will! Shall I tell the story Tia or do you still want to?'

'You tell a story better than me so yes go ahead,' Tia explained as she gave up on her last piece of pizza and returned it to the box.

'Yes so, when Apollonia contested the will it was a very long process. There had been evidence that she had stayed at the kafenion from witnesses living nearby who had seen her going in and out at the most strangest of times. The letters that my uncle had supposedly written were taken into account but then were misplaced at the lawyers. And so it went on and on —one delay after another. In the end, the lawyer suggested we pay her off but we decided not to so it went on for another two years. It sounds awful but we were thinking that with her old age her mind might have become senile but instead, her mind was as strong as a mountain goat!' Andreas relayed as the three women smiled.

A Lock up on Crete

'Ladies, did I use the wrong expression?'

'It's good, we understand. Maybe if you use this expression – *her mind was as sharp as a pin,*' Zoe explained, not wanting to sound condescending. After all, who was she to correct someone's English? She wished sometimes Andreas's generation hadn't spoken English so well and then she would have been forced to learn more Greek. She reminded herself to ask Tia how long it had taken her to learn Greek. Andreas mulled over the new phrase as Tia continued the story.

'Anyway, about a year later, the witnesses were called forward again. The three female witnesses had switched their allegiance and somehow came up with the evidence that Apollonia had been visiting the kafenion as a prostitute!'

'Oh my God!' Both Zoe and her mother exclaimed as her mother glanced at the locket on Zoe's neck.

'But how old would she have been then?' asked an astounded Eve.

'About sixty as she is now about ninety,' added Andreas visibly reckoning up in his head.

'I'm just sorry my uncle had to resort to the comfort of Apollonia,' Andreas replied as Zoe switched the focus, realising that Andreas was clearly upset for his late uncle.

'Well, at least your uncle would have been proud that you and Tia received what was rightfully yours. Oh sorry, I am assuming you did inherit the kafenion though?' Zoe corrected herself as her mother cleared the small plates onto the trolley.

A Lock up on Crete

'Ahhh, yes. My uncle's wealth was clearly more than any of us imagined and my sisters and parents shared with us the plentiful inheritance. Tia and I took over the traditional kafenion but we changed with the times and it is now a snack bar to cater for the younger generation. We own it and my niece and her husband manage it as we decided to stay in Iraepetra, near to my parents,' Andreas explained as Tia fondly looked at her husband. Zoe was dying to ask whether they inherited the small cottage with the most enviable view of Mirabello Bay but knew not to probe any further- there had been enough revelations for the day, she reminded herself. She also couldn't help but wonder if they received any compensation for the accident resulting in Andreas's limp. Zoe also pondered why, if they had a bit of cash behind them, they had stayed in the small apartment with the awful stairway. Maybe they enjoyed waking up each morning to the sight, sounds and smell of the sea. That was worth more than any flash villa inland, she mused.

The last bus back to Iraepetra was at 8pm. Andreas had found out from a quick call to his friend.
'Oh wow it's six already! And we have to get to Elounda from Agios Nikolaos so I think we ought to get the 7pm bus.' Zoe reasoned, realising all the alcohol and the sudden surprise had taken it out of Andreas as he stifled a yawn.
'It's been absolutely amazing,' said Tia as she gave Zoe and Eve a massive hug and kiss and sent them on their way with a paper bag of local cherries. Andreas followed

A Lock up on Crete

suit with a plastic water bottle of raki, which to refuse, would be a cardinal sin.

'Zoe, please don't leave it for another thirty one year's please and it was lovely meeting you Eve,' Andreas excused himself from going down the stairs to see them out.

'We will definitely be back won't we Mum?'

'Absolutley, it's a beautiful island and I even like that Raki drink!' Eve replied as they hugged once more and waved up to the balcony to Andreas.

As mother and daughter sat on the bus waiting to depart, Eve broached some questions that she had collected during the reunion.

'Zoe dear, I wonder why they don't have any children? It just seems strange with them being in a catholic country like this and seeing how much children are revered. Oh and that Apollo woman – what a witch! And to think that she was still selling herself at that age!' Zoe smiled at the questions that were mulling through her mother's inquisitive mind.

'Well seeing as though this is the first time I've seen them since 1984 I don't know about the children but I did think the same myself to be honest. And I would be very surprised if Apollonia is still selling herself but then again she never failed to shock. Anyway, there was so much to take in today so it will be a good excuse to return. What do you think Mum?'

'Absolutley! I adore Crete. I can't believe your father and I never visited Greece to be honest. He would have loved the colour of that sea for sure. Oh it was so interesting today with Tia and Andreas.' Both women became lost in their own thoughts as the bus pulled out onto the national road to Agios Nikolaos. Soon, they were both snoozing and only woke when the conductor announced in a sing song voice, Agios, Agios, Agios Nikolaos. Fortunately, their connecting bus was just about to leave as they hopped on board and settled down for another half an hour journey to Elounda.

Chapter 2

Elounda, Last day of Zoe and Eve's visit

Eve was taking an afternoon nap as a result of the previous night's indulgence in a fair few cocktails. Their coach transfer was due to take them back to Heraklion airport at 8pm.
Zoe couldn't settle so decided to go for a last stroll up and down Elounda to tire herself a little. She left a note for her mum and made her way down the small hill to the big supermarket where she hoped to buy a few souvenirs. She peered into a low tree trying to see what the cicadas looked like that made their chaotic chorus in the afternoon heat. It was almost as though these transparent creatures were protesting against anyone who thought they could take a siesta.
Just before the supermarket, a man stood outside his shop and wished her kalispera as she replied the same. A photo of an abandoned house in the shop window caught her eye as she bent a little to look closer at it.

A Lock up on Crete

'You are interested in buying here in Crete? This house is near Elounda. It is very expensive in Elounda but this house is up in one of our rustic villages. Come inside and take a look at some more,' he gestured showing her a seat. It tickled her how the Greeks seemed to ask so many questions and answers all in the same breath as she still hadn't given him a reply. Yes would have been her response to his first question if only she could afford it and yes she might as well go inside where it was a bit cooler. There was no harm in looking she thought.

'I am Angelino and your name is?'

'Oh sorry yes I am Zoe, me lene Zoe.'

'Ahhh you speak a little Greek,' Angelino smiled.

'Ligo, ligo,' Zoe admitted as she continued to look at the picture of the abandoned house which, with the right investment, could make her dream about owning a little house come true.

'Now this house you look at it is very cheap, only 25,000 euros. I can take you now if you like. The owner is not living and the son is in Athens so I can show you round now.'

Before she had really thought about it, Zoe took her place in the passenger seat in the air conditioned car leaving the pretty fishing village of Elounda behind. As they climbed the mountain road, they passed villages that seemed to be abandoned as if everyone had fled a civil war or such like. Old wooden doors hung limply from their hinges and window frames screamed out for a lick of paint.

'This village,' she asked Angelino as he turned his radio down, 'Is it abandoned?'

A Lock up on Crete

'No, no, why you ask? Look over there. That is the village barber and he works at his house there,' Angelino pointed to a small house that had a sign on in Greek which must have said Barber. The man looked up as if he knew he was being talked about. They slowed down a little to where she could see he was cleaning his scissors in some solution on the stone step of his shop and home. Next to his house lay piles of rusted scrap metal and what looked like an old tin bath. Zoe was mesmerised how they could live alongside the relics from yesteryear. She realised that maybe up in these villages there was no refuse collection so they had to store it themselves.

No sooner than the thought had come to her, Angelino pomped his horn as a refuse truck thundered past, narrowly missing his wing mirror. Angelino gestured with his thumb and sounded some profanities as they left the village onto the mountain road which took them over to the village of Pines.

'Ah it is a pretty village and a nice name,' Zoe remarked as Angelino nodded and corrected her pronunciation of Pines, stressing each syllable equally with the outcome sounding like P EE N I S. She supressed a giggle, then felt foolish as they parked up in the tiniest bit of shade they could find and entered the property through the bramble choked courtyard. They climbed the rickety metal steps to the upper floor which still had some sort of weaving machine in the corner and various icon pictures hanging lopsided on the wall. The balcony had seen better days as Angelino promptly stopped Zoe from stepping on to.

A Lock up on Crete

'Yes or no?' he asked as they returned to the car.

'Do you know of any properties in need of repair but smaller and a smaller cost? I have seen them on other websites before I came here on holiday and they look like they are some kind of outbuildings,' Zoe asked, realising that she really should be returning to her mother in Elounda. She sent a quick text to her telling her not to worry and that she would be back soon in time for their last meal and cocktail of the holiday. Angelino smiled from ear to ear as he spun the car around and headed inland.

'Ahhh I do have one. It is in my village. Come I take you.'

'Is it far? I have to return soon. We are flying back tonight.'

'No no, it is on our way. I think you may like this Zoe,' he assured her, turning up the radio and singing along to the up tempo bouzouki music as he tapped the beat on the steering wheel.

'This is my village,' he proudly declared as they arrived at the bottom of the mountain road close to the national road.

'Wow it is very traditional and pretty,' she exclaimed as they passed an older man guiding his donkey with his wife riding side saddle. She recalled the souvenir shops in Elounda with the same postcards of the same image. She smiled yet again as the man waved and smiled to them and his wife scowled in return. They pulled up in the centre of the village as Angelino explained the car was too wide for the cobbled lanes. They walked the extra few hundred yards, passing children as they

A Lock up on Crete

screamed (or probably just talked) at each other. As if to read her thoughts, Angelino pointed beyond the olive groves to buildings in the distance.

'Our large town of Neapoli. Here you can buy most things you cannot in my village like hardware things and there is also a college and a prison.' He said the word prison like he was proud of the fact it stood right next to the national road and could also be seen from many directions; its purpose to warn any troublemakers, regardless that although the sun shone for most of the year on the island, it certainly didn't shine in any of the cells.

'Yes I know Neapoli,' she replied as Angelino threw her a confused look.

'If only he knew,' she mused as she followed him to a dead end where he pulled a rotten wooden door aside to reveal a stone storage building. Zoe continued behind him as he shone his torch inside, warding off any creature that had made it their home.

'Look at the arches Zoe. This is good building. This is nice to be a home with a little renovation. You like it Zoe, yes or no?'

'I do like it very much. It has a sweet smell in here but do you think it could be converted to a holiday home?'

'I am without doubt it can be. It is mine Zoe. I am the owner and I can tell you for a little price you can make it your home with these amazing views over my valley.'

Lost in her thoughts, Zoe pondered on the situation and why, after all these years she had only just returned to her beloved Crete. As she was now single and her children had flown the nest, she asked herself, was she

really brave enough to invest in a little piece of Crete.
She didn't have much money but maybe it wouldn't take
much money to buy and renovate. She answered herself
with a resounding Yes!

'How much Angelino?'

'Ahhh I think you are a genuinely in love with my country
so I will offer it to you for 10,000 euros.'

'I will return to the UK and get in touch with you. I have a
lot of maths to do Angelino.'

After shutting the door as best he could on the little
storage shed, Zoe cast a final sweep over the abundant
valley and knew what she really wanted.

Back on the road, heading in the opposite direction
toward Neapoli, Angelino pointed.

'Zoe, Zoe. Here is the prison of the prefecture of Lasitthi.
There are only two prisons on the whole of the island;
the other one is near Chania. Oh and did you see the sign
for Malia? Did you see the bullet holes in it? Well do not
be worried it is nothing but the locals using their guns.
Did you know that most people have a gun licence and
own guns on Crete but please do not worry as gun crime
is very, very low. If you decide to buy my house, well
there are a lot of ex pats living nearby. You will not be
lonely.'

Zoe thought it was about time to tell him some home
truths so as to alert him to the fact that he couldn't pull
the wool over her eyes so to speak. From her past
experiences she knew already how filoxenia ran through
the Cretan's veins but best be on guard all the same.

A Lock up on Crete

'Angelino, I was here in Crete in 1984 mostly in Iraepetra. My English friend who I came with still lives in Iraepetra with her Greek husband. I have just seen them for the first time in thirty one years. I know this side of the island quite well,' Zoe revealed as Angelino took his eyes off the road for far too long.

'Po Po Po!' This is a nice story. So if you would like to buy my house you need to decide soon as I have many Europeans interested in it and as you can see it is an amazing view over the olive groves.'

'Thank you Angelino for showing me your stone building. I will take your email and reply soon with my answer but I need to return to my mother and not be late for our airport transfer. Efcharisto poli Angelino.'

'Parakalo,' Angelino pumped Zoe's hand enthusiastically as she opened the car door and entered the dated but perfectly positioned hotel. They had been lucky to have a room overlooking the whole of Mirabello Bay; a view she knew she would never tire of.

'It's a shame we have to go home tonight,' Eve reflected as she packed the last few items in her case. 'I would like to have seen this property.' Zoe had relayed her chance meeting and impromptu trip with Angelino.

'I'm glad you like it here mum,' Zoe wondered whether to check if they could change their flights and stay longer to show her mother the stone building but decided that they could return soon – another excuse to savour all the flavours that the magical island had to offer.

A Lock up on Crete

Chapter 3

<u>Zoe, Late August 2015 UK</u>

Within a day of returning from Crete, Zoe had sent the email.

Hello Angelino
I would like to make you an offer for the stone building you own for the sum of 8,000 euros.
Thank you
Zoe Matthews

Hello Zoe
I have the house on the market for 10,000 euros but I would like to sell to you at 9,500 euros.
Yours
Angelino

Hello Angelino
As the stone building will need a lot of money spent on it to make it into a house I can offer you 8,000 euro
However, this is subject to my mother Eve approving.
Yours
Zoe

Hello Zoe
Because I like your story from the time you were in Crete many years ago, I will sell you my house for 8500 euros.

A Lock up on Crete

I hope to see you soon. You will be also buying your
house in a recognised traditional Cretan village with
many beautiful view.
Yours
Angelino

England September 2015

'Ok Zoe, I think it would be a good idea if I came back
out to Crete with you soon and had a look at this little
building or whatever it is you have fallen in love with.'
'Oh, Mum that would be great. If you don't approve or
think it's going to be too much of a money pit then I will
follow your advice. I'll look at flights now,' said Zoe while
accepting another slice of her mother's lemon drizzle
cake.

By the end of the day they had booked flights and some
accommodation for four days. That would give them
enough time to look at the outbuilding again and
arrange lawyers if her mother approved. Zoe couldn't
contain her excitement but knew she had to think clearly
and think of all the possible dilemmas and scenarios.

October 2015

'Ahh, kalimera, kalimera,' greeted Angelino as he shook
Zoe's hand first then her mothers.
'Kalimera Angelino. Please meet my mother.' Angelino
looked more relaxed than he had in the summer when
he was busy selling million euro properties to the
plethora of Russian oligarchs that seemed to be buying
up much of the Elounda property. It was his son's estate

agent but as Angelino had officially retired he had helped him set it all up and by the looks of things had taken a front seat on the running of it.

'Hello Angelino. Pleased to meet you,' said Eve as she shielded her eyes from the low autumnal sunshine. They were soon at the traditional village as Angelino parked his car in the shade next to a large church. Zoe watched as her mother surveyed the church as she always did upon seeing one. She was probably itching to take a look inside and light a few candles.

'Please Zoe and Zoe's mama, follow me.'

'Sorry Angelino I forgot to introduce you properly. Mitera mou, se lene Eve.'

'Ahh Eve a very nice name. Ok Zoe and mother Eve, please follow.' Both women stepped in line and followed Angelino through a maze of small passage ways, passing little stone houses which looked abandoned but probably weren't. Zoe thought back to the village on the way to the first property in Pines that Angelino had taken her to.

'Nearly at the house,' Angelino smiled as he swept plump grapes hanging from their vines out of their path. The bougainvillea was still abundant and carpeted the stone walls in pink and purple hues.

After a few more twists and turns they arrived at Angelino's little stone building. Angelino turned the key in the lock of the battered wooden door as a heady scent hit them from within. It was a mixture of years of dampness and the aroma of some kind of spice, maybe cinnamon.

A Lock up on Crete

Zoe's mother quietly surveyed the natural stone building before nodding her approval to Zoe while Angelino checked the roof which was in need of repair. It was about 40m2 on one level with two impressive stone arches dividing what could be potential rooms.

'And now you have seen my house, what do you think Zoe's mama?' Angelino asked as he absently stroked the smooth stone on the arches.

'Leave it with me Angelino please,' Eve said as Zoe could see the confusion in Angelino's eyes with the phrase. 'We mean we have to talk about the money before we go to the lawyer. We will see you tomorrow and will be able to give you a final answer.' Zoe sensed the confusion with Angelino – after all she had near but confirmed the purchase in the emails she had sent but she knew she had to fully discuss it with her mother before the final answer. Looking a little disappointed, Angelino nodded as he locked up and led the way back through the colourful little alleyway.

'I think you will enjoy living in my village,' Angelino said as he swept his arm like a clock face across his village. To the right, their eyes met with the impressive church onto the olive groves and to the left the village buildings, some whitewashed, others still baring their original stone and all bursting with the vivid colours of vines and flowers.

Agios Nikolaos
Zoe and Eve

A Lock up on Crete

Early the next morning Zoe woke with a start as her mother placed a cup of milky coffee on her bedside table.

'Are you ok Zoe? You look as though you've seen a ghost!'

'Oh, I just had a weird dream. I always do when I am on holiday. It's nothing,' she reassured her mother who continued with her morning routine of cleansing, toning and moisturising her face and neck. Zoe felt like all her energy had been sucked from her body as she lay back on her pillow.

Apollonia and Cara had visited her in her dream. But instead of an old lady in her widow weeds, Apollonia had morphed into a younger woman. The woman was unmistakably Cara, Cara Matthews - dressed in a white wedding dress. She stood by the grave of Old Manolis Mariakis. Around her neck, hung Zoe's locket. Then her youthful features faded into the creased face of Apollonia

The Lawyer

Zoe felt a tingle down her spine as she entered the lawyer's office. Immediately, Zoe and her mother were made to feel welcome and a coffee was promptly ordered. She was shown to a chair at the lawyer's desk while her mother sat on a comfy sofa behind and was handed her first ever Frappe coffee. She took a sip and winced, much to the amusement of the lawyer.

A Lock up on Crete

'Ahh so this is your first Frappe?' he said, while organising some files on his desk.

'Yes it is. I think it might grow on me,' Eve assured, paranoid of offending anyone. The lawyer who introduced himself as Tyrone, explained the English idiom to Angelino who sat opposite Zoe.

'Ahhh, Yes, I understand. I find your English sayings funny and not so funny,' Angelino commented as they all smiled before the seriousness of the meeting.

'Ok, so, we will proceed. First I need to talk you through my lawyer practice and costs. Then I will listen to you as you tell me everything about your offer to buy the property from my good friend here Angelino Andrianakis.'

Zoe touched her temples as she tried to focus on what the lawyer was translating for her. She felt out of her depth. Her mother picked up on her daughter's distress and handed her a blister pack of painkillers.

'Miss Matthews. Are you ill?' the lawyer stopped his spiel abruptly.

'Just a small headache,' her mother explained as he nodded and continued at a slower pace.

Zoe continued the meeting by relaying to the lawyer her first meeting with Angelino and the subsequent viewing of the property with her mother.

'Do you have any concerns about the legal side Miss Matthews?' the lawyer asked as he maintained eye contact.

'Please call me Zoe and my mother, Eve. Yes. There are a few things I would like clarification on. You see there are a lot of programmes we watch in the UK about people

A Lock up on Crete

buying abroad and the pitfalls and buying a property which is not actually legal.'

'Ahh this is only a natural concern and is one which I also would worry a little if I bought a property, maybe in your country. So here, let me show you the searches you must complete and we will conduct them on your behalf. Also, I will act as your Power of Attorney which we will have to conduct with the Notary soon.' Although Tyrone, who Eve couldn't help but think of the same named character in the hit soap, Coronation St, spoke with great clarity, Zoe began to lose focus again as she looked at her mother to gauge her thoughts and expression. If her mother felt assured by the well-mannered lawyer then that would be enough for Zoe. After all, Zoe knew her mother was a good judge of character. With all the preliminary paperwork completed and with the assurance that the whole purchase should go smoothly as the property belonged to Angelino, they made an appointment for the next day to meet again at the Notary in Neapoli.

A short walk from Tyrone's office was a well- stocked supermarket as both women perused the aisles and bought trinkets to take home, including a bright wall plaque of two Cretan fishermen standing before a blue sea which Eve bought for Zoe. No trip was complete without indulging in souvenir shopping her mother reminded her.

The following morning they made their way up to the bus station, once again passing the ever picturesque lake and further up, the large hospital.

A Lock up on Crete

'Is that a market over there Zoe?' Eve pointed to the colourful stands that had taken over a section of abandoned land near the hospital car park.
'It looks like it Mum. I think it is a fruit and veg market.' As they neared the market it seemed like they had entered into a giant world. There were watermelons quite literally as huge as watermelons; massive beef tomatoes; gigantic ears of corn and even the purple hued cherries looked like baubles on a Christmas tree. Eve bought a punnet for their bus journey as the vendor poured some water over them and handed her a few napkins with an enormous smile as Eve reciprocated. 'Efcharisto poli,' she added as Zoe nodded her head in approval.

The bus station was busy as usual as Zoe scanned the digital timetable for the next bus to Neapoli. Eve remarked how efficient she found the public transport compared to back home. Zoe explained that the buses were mostly family businesses and thus took great pride in their coaches, promptness and very reasonable fares. They just had enough time to grab a tiropita cheese pie each from the small taverna opposite the station. Zoe wondered whether this was the taverna that had bought the bakewell tarts that Mel used to bake for the ex- pat as she spotted a few paler -faced middle aged, men sipping tea from cups and saucer.

They were an hour early for their meeting with the Notary as they sipped a coffee at one of the café bars lining the main square of Neapoli. Eve watched the

A Lock up on Crete

school children as they arrived back from school off the buses. Zoe checked her phone to check in with her two grown up children who were both travelling in different parts of the globe while her mother checked her watch. 'It's only 1pm,' she commented as the loud children dispersed to their homes in every direction.

'It's Friday so they probably finish early,' Zoe suggested as she looked across at the Law Courts. She had decided to tell her mother her story but hesitated not quite knowing how to broach the subject: Her mother broke her thoughts.

'Just look at that church Zoe! Look at how it dominates the town. Have we got time to have a quick peep in?' No sooner had the words left her mouth, when around every corner and alleyway, entered a procession of people, singing and holding up icons of the Blessed Virgin. Two coaches also pulled up as throngs of pilgrims descended on the town square dressed in bright colours with the women shielding their heads with scarves.

'Ladies, please allow me to explain,' the waiter announced as he handed them a leaflet and sat down opposite.

'This is your first time to Neapoli, no?'

'Yes and no really,' Zoe replied realising what a stupid answer it was. The waiter dismissed her reply and pointed to the leaflet.

'Today 15th August each year is the celebration of our beautiful Megali Panagia church – Great Holy Virgin Mary. It is the largest in Eastern Crete and today is dedicated to the Dormition of Theotokos. These pilgrims you see have travelled from all over Crete, some never having left their villages all year.' Eve was riveted as she politely interrupted his flow.

'Forgive me for interrupting but of course I should have remembered. Today is the feast of the Assumption of the Virgin Mary – her falling asleep and her bodily resurrection before being taken up into heaven.'

'You are a Christian no?' the waiter asked as he unconsciously stacked the coffee cups.

'Yes we are Catholic. Do you think we could enter the church?' Eve replied as her eyes followed the throng of pilgrims as the heavy doors opened and the first wave of worshippers muscled their way in to show their respects.

'Of course you can but be warned it may take a while before the crowds become less.' The waiter hesitated as if he wanted to tell them more. He sat down again.

'Please as you are interested allow me to tell you more of the churches history.' Zoe looked at her watch and nodded having another fifteen minutes spare. Eve ordered another coffee as she rose to take a photo of the town of Neapoli, resplendent with celebration.

The waiter returned with more coffee and two glasses of cold water.

'So my boss says I can sit with you for another five minutes as it is important for visitors to understand our important town. Neapoli was the regional unit of this area of Crete: that is why over there are the Law Courts and overlooking the town to your left you see the watch tower of the prison!' Despite the brightness, the waiter opened his eyes wide at his last comment before continuing. His voice became louder as he competed

A Lock up on Crete

with the loud chanting and singing - Zoe and Eve moved closer to him.

'Ok so our church has a rich story to tell. In tradition, in 1891 three members of the committee of the church went to Istanbul which was maybe known as Constantinople then, I am not very sure of that but anyways they went to ask for a Firman which is financing by the Turkish authorities as the Turks ruled our land then. Anyways, they asked to build a temple on the site which had been ruined. Instead of a Firman, the Turkish officer gave a sealed envelope to the three committee members to be delivered to Heraklion. Heraklion is our capital city and back then may have been called Chandia - I am not so sure and maybe I should have paid more attention to my school history lessons!' His wide eyes narrowed as he smiled and took a sip of water. Both women remained silent, hoping he would finish his story in time. 'Anyways, the sealed envelope not contained the Firman but an order to hang the three members to death!'

'Oh my God,' Eve announced as she crossed herself instinctively – a Greek trait she was using more and more.

'So the officer opened the envelope and sent the three members to prison. One day before the hanging the executioner died of a heart attack. The commander considered it a bad omen and allowed the rebuilding of the temple but it had to be built within 40 days. Christians from the surrounding provinces willingly offered to build it so volunteers and locals transferred the stones hand by hand from the quarry to the church

A Lock up on Crete

within the 40 days and then it was inaugurated by the Bishop of Petra who was then murdered by the Turks in 1821. Oh ladies I must go back to work now. Please visit the church when the madness has gone.'

'Wow! That was a whistle stop tour of Neapoli!' declared Zoe as she checked her watch and realised why the animosity between the Greeks and Turks still was evident and rooted in anger.

'Did the nice waiter just say the three men were spared from death, Zoe?'

'Yes he did. 'Come on Mum we better find this Notary office and hopefully we can have a look at the church after.'

'Ok dear, I better just pop to the loo.' On her return Eve passed the waiter who confirmed the three men had definitely been spared. She crossed herself again feeling more content and joined her daughter.

Angelino was already in the cool office as he stood up to greet them.

'Ahh, Zoe's mama, Eve. Have you come to a decision about my house?'

'Yes I have and although it is not really my say anyway, I do think my daughter has always felt a connection with Crete. So I feel it in my bones that she should buy it and have her little piece of your wonderful island.'

Zoe could tell that Angelino hadn't fully understood her mother but felt assured she had good people behind her to make her dream a reality.

Zoe signed the final document as Eve, Angelino and the Notary shook her hand and nodded their approval.

A Lock up on Crete

Back in the town square, both mother and daughter felt
a reluctance to leave as they sat on a stone bench set in
a small garden area. Opposite them, juxtaposed with the
ornate church, the sight of the imposing Law Court of
Neapoli took Zoe's breath away. She cast her mind back
some thirty years previously when she had first entered
those same tall, steel doors – a petrified twenty year old
English girl in a foreign country.

'Mum, you see that building?'

'Yes Zoe. I see it. What is it?'

'Ok here goes Mum. Firstly, did you see that building on
the roadside just before we turned off for Neapoli?'

'No I didn't to be honest,' Eve replied.

'Well, like the waiter explained, it is the prison and just
there are the Law Courts.' Eve widened her eyes as if to
prompt her daughter to get to the point, itching for the
crowds to disperse so they could enter the church.

'Mum, I have something to tell you from when I was first
here.'

'Oh my God, don't tell me you went to prison all those
years ago?'

'No, no Mum. Of course I didn't. Well I I went to the Law
Courts but not the prison.'

'Phew,' Eve let out a sigh as Zoe continued.

'In 1985, when I came back home from Crete I was
mentally exhausted and also sick with worry that you
would ask where my locket was. I couldn't tell you the
whole story of why I had returned earlier than I had
planned because I didn't want to worry you. I still had
the travel bug in me so I shielded you from the truth.

A Lock up on Crete

Anyway Mum, here is the story of the trip to Istanbul and the Law courts...' Zoe told her story as her mother listened, nodding and shaking her head as her daughter's story unfolded. Eve imparted a few gasps and many sign of the crosses as she looked over at the Law Courts, imagining her precious daughter having to endure the court hearing in a foreign language. She wondered what she would have been doing back home while her daughter was feeling out of her depth and scared for her life. Her memory raced back to the year of 1984. She remembered just having received an air mail letter from Zoe and re reading it at her kitchen table while putting the finishing touches on her lemon drizzle cake ready for the village fete the following day. She also remembered how the next day as she gathered her exhibits for the competition which included her lemon drizzle cake, her Victoria sponge cake and a small sweet pea flower arrangement she had lovingly created, that another air mail envelope had dropped through the letterbox as she put it aside, reminding herself to read it on her return. It had been addressed to Zoe so she would send it on to her. However, Eve, still revelling from the 2 'first' places she had won hands down, clean forgot about the letter for Zoe - only to be found again thirty one years later! If only her daughter had told her what was happening in Crete, she could have flown over and been there for her.

'So what do you think then Mum?' Eve took a few moments to compose herself, her gaze fixated on the beautiful church opposite
'Mum, Mum, can you hear me?'

A Lock up on Crete

'Yes dear I can hear you. What did you ask?'

'About me testifying in those courts in 1984, Zoe clarified, wondering if her mother had even been listening.

'Yes, yes. I heard what you told me Zoe and to be honest there's not a lot that shocks me these days. I'm not surprised you didn't tell me at the time! You probably knew I was worrying enough when I couldn't always get in touch with you and I didn't know where you were. After all, there were no mobile phones then were there? Just the telephone exchanges and post restante!' Eve half smiled at her daughter as she wondered what revelation she would come up with next.

'Yes you would have had me on the next plane home no doubt!' Zoe added as she followed her mother over to the steps of the church.

'I would have come to collect you myself!' Eve sighed as instead of crossing herself again she raised both palms in front of her face. Zoe giggled as she thought how easy her mother was picking up the Greek traits and mannerisms.

'Yes and I'm probably the same with my two kids I suppose. Wow! Can you imagine not having mobile phones and other technology now?' Both women shook their heads as they strolled over to the church. Zoe felt a weight had been lifted from her shoulders as she confidently walked past the Law Courts without any of the shivers she had previously. They climbed the few steps of the church and gazed at the modern frescoes and bright dome. They opened the huge door with caution as a herd of pilgrims bolted into the bright

A Lock up on Crete

August sunshine as both women scuttled for shelter in the recesses.

Back in the UK, November 2015

Zoe opened the email from Angelino.
Dear Zoe and mother Eve
It was a pleasure to sell you my house to you and I hope to see you both soon so we can look at how best to make it your Cretan home.
Angelino

Her heart raced as she opened up another one from her lawyer, Tyrone.
'Mum I have just received the Deeds to the stone outbuilding in Crete!' Zoe yelled down the phone.
'Fantastic! Do you have to call it an outbuilding though Zoe? Angelino even referred to it as a house if I remember.'
'Yes you're right again Mum. I'll have a think of what to name it. Oh hang on there's some post just come through the letter box.'
Eve waited as she sipped her cup of tea and dunked a biscuit while she waited for her daughter to open her mail. She watched from her sunny conservatory as the neighbour's cat chased a squirrel up a tree.
'Zoe, Zoe. Are you still there?'
'Yes! I just received the hard copy of the Deeds and building permission from the lawyer to the Lock Up!'

A Lock up on Crete

'Oh yes that is an apt name for it - A Lock Up . I take it you mean a property you can lock up till your next visit and not the prison you came quite close to in 1984?'

'Of course it's a lock up as in a house Mum. I'm older and wiser now!'

Both women laughed then made a date to meet up to discuss a plan of action to bring the little Lock- Up in Crete to fruition.

'Oh and Mum. I got a message from Mel this morning to say she is coming back to visit her sister next summer. We can make our dream of a reunion real and visit Tia and Andreas.

'That would be lovely love. Three friends reunited at last.' Eve reflected.

'You're coming too Mum!'

May 2015 Agios Nikolaos, Zoe and Tia

Tia scanned the bus that had arrived from Heraklion. Likewise, Zoe scanned the bus station for Tia. They spotted each other and waved frantically.

'Yassoo - it's so good to see you again,' they shrilled as they embraced.

They walked the short distance down to the Snak Stop where Tia delivered their employees weekly wages.

'Just leave your backpack there Zoe and we'll come back later,' Tia instructed as she spoke in Greek to her nephew in law and handed over the small brown envelopes.

'Are you sure it's ok for me to stay upstairs at the Snak Stop Tia?'

A Lock up on Crete

'Yes of course it is but let's leave it till later,' she said as she directed Zoe out of the small shop onto the pavement. Zoe glanced back and was transported back to October 1984 when the three of them had first arrived and taken their first fateful step into the kafenion of old Manolis Mariakis. All too soon, she was shaken out of her reverie.

'Come on day dreamer. Let's have a beer!' Tia announced as they walked down the hill to the waterfront tavernas. They ordered a beer each and settled down in the director style chairs next to the fishing boats. Zoe was still in amazed how the young waiters and waitresses swiftly made it from one side to the other side of the road with trays of orders, without being run over.

Tia cut to the chase.

'Apollonia is still living above the launderette I've been told but I had a look earlier and I can't actually see any entrance to the upper floor unless we go through the launderette itself.' Tia imparted as she scooped a handful of nuts from the small bowl.

Zoe had told Tia about her recurring dream and how she wanted closure on the truth about how the locket had come to be in Apollonia's possession.

'Well do you think we should just walk in then and ask for her?' Zoe asked her friend as they ordered another beer each.

'I think you should go in first and ask whoever is working there and then we will take it from there.' Tia suggested as she caught the attention of the waiter for the bill.

A Lock up on Crete

The launderette hadn't changed at all and still had the same colour walls and tiled floor, peppered with white washing powder.

'Can I help you?' a young teenage girl asked Zoe in a clipped English accent as she loaded a machine.

'Hello. Yes I am looking for a lady called Apollonia,' Zoe replied as she recognised something in the way the young girl with the jet black bobbed hair tilted her head to the right.

'Apollonia? Yes, Apollonia was my father's aunt. Who did you say you were?'

Zoe was grounded to the spot. So Apollonia must have died then, Zoe thought as she wondered who the young girl's father was.

'Daddy lived here once but I live in England now. I'm just here on holiday. I'll call her down if you like,' the young girl said as she shouted in Greek through the door to the stairs. Zoe still couldn't quite grasp whether Apollonia was dead or alive and why the young girl was explaining herself to her so much.

Tia looked on from a distance.

Apollonia appeared a short time later from the steep stairs.

'Pios ine? Koritsi mou?'

'I don't know aunty but she asked for you and she speaks in English.'

'Can I help you my dear?' Apollonia's voice was quiet and crackly as she rested her old body on a wooden stool. Feeling as though she was living the recurring dream and Apollonia was merely a figment of her imagination, Zoe drew a deep breath in the hope that

A Lock up on Crete

her well- rehearsed spiel would have the impact she hoped for.

'Yes I am here to ask you about a locket. This locket,' Zoe took the locket from her neck and rested it in her palm. Apollonia and the young girl said something in Greek to each other and shrugged their shoulders.

'Apollonia, this is the locket that you took to my friend Tia and her husband Andreas for repair many years ago. '

'And so what is this anything to do with my father's aunt?' the young girl asked with folded arms.

'Po, po, po. My locket!' Apollonia exclaimed as her great niece moved in closer to her great aunt.

Tia walked in and mouthed 'are you ok' to Zoe. Zoe nodded as she took a step back and continued to speak. 'No Apollonia. It is my locket and I would like to know who gave it to you.' Zoe carefully opened it and revealed the two sets of photos. 'These are my parents but I don't know who these babies are,' Zoe explained, as Apollonia took Damianos' daughter's hand to steady herself. The young girl spoke rapidly in Greek as Apollonia nodded and wiped a tear away.

'My memory is fading but this locket was given to me by my beautiful nephew. The babies are Damianos and his brother. I miss him so much. He was my life.' Apollonia broke down as the young girl comforted her and threw a cautionary look at Zoe. Tia intervened and explained more in Greek.

'Damianos died a few years ago in England. This is his daughter, Andrea,' Tia relayed to Zoe. Before Andrea helped her great aunt back up to her room, Apollonia asked to hold the locket one last time. All four women

A Lock up on Crete

welled up as the little old lady kissed the photo of the babies and gave the locket back to Zoe. Zoe took the photos out and placed them in Apollonia's withered hand.

'Here, he is back with you now,' Zoe whispered. 'And I am really sorry for your loss,' she added as the old lady and her great niece took the first step of the stairs.

'How do you feel?' Tia asked Zoe as they walked around the harbour and stopped at a modern sculpture of a stone horn – the Horn of Almathea.

'I feel sad and relieved. Sad that Damianos has died at such an early age and relieved that I have found out that it was him who stole the locket. I also feel sorry for his daughter who is so like him in looks and mannerisms but hopefully she is a better person than her father.

'Yes very true. Damianos spoiled himself that's for sure but maybe he was a good role model to his daughter before he died,' Tia chipped in as she followed the steel Horn of Amalthea up to the blue sky.

'Do you know much about this sculpture, Tia? It's really cool.'

'No I don't really. I must ask Andreas or just Google it – the easier option I guess.' Both friends nodded in agreement at how the internet had taken over the world and the power of questioning.

'Sorry I digressed then. Yes I also feel relieved that I have made peace with Apollonia to be honest. I'm sure she must have had quite a hard life really; especially if she had to resort to selling herself, which still kind of baffles me.'

A Lock up on Crete

'Me too. She must have enjoyed it maybe? She might have liked the control and power it brought her,' Tia concluded as both friends took a seat at the bottom of the horn sculpture and had a minute of silence.

'I wonder how he died? And I wonder who he married? I can't believe it wasn't spoken about in Iraepetra. I must find out when I go back. Maybe his parents are both dead too and his siblings have never revealed that he died. I'll find out when I'm next in the salon and let you know.'

'Yes, please do. I did have a soft spot for him even after all that we went through. I really hope he was a good father and husband. And I hope he mended his ways in his later years,' Zoe reflected as Tia took her hand and pulled her up from the stone seat. They linked arms as they walked around to Kitroplatia beach where they had first ventured down to, all those years ago with Mel in the lead and Apollonia keeping her beady eyes on them from afar.

'When I spoke in Greek, Andrea said her father met her mother in London and they have been there ever since. I don't know how he died though but he must have a memorial here as Andrea said she had been to lay flowers and comes to spend most of her school holidays here visiting Apollonia and earning a bit of cash in the launderette.' Tia explained as the little horseshoe beach came into view from around the corner of the headland. 'You know dreams really do come true don't they Tia? 'What do you mean Zoe?'

A Lock up on Crete

'Well that recurring dream I told you about. Apollonia was dressed in a white wedding dress but she kept morphing into Cara and then back again. She had my locket and was standing at a grave. I just don't know why Cara was in it though,' Zoe sighed as Tia led her to another statue of the abduction of Europa by Zeus. Both women breathed in the pure Cretan air and closed their eyes. Tia broke the silence after a few minutes of reflection.

'You know, we never did keep in touch with Cara did we? I wonder what happened to her?'

'Maybe still with the man from Milan?' Zoe added with a chuckle.

'I never did trust her to be honest,' Tia opened her palms and turned her mouth down; a Cretan mannerism she had surely perfected over the years. Zoe shrugged her shoulders as a beautiful pink hue lit up the mountains opposite from the sinking sun. Zoe's time in Crete was coming to an end. But not for long!

Epilogue

Late August 2015
Heraklion Airport

'Noooooo! Mel, Mel, it really is Meli mou! Tia screeched as Andreas covered his ears. Zoe greeted Andreas as Tia and Mel flung themselves at each other, ruffling each other's hair as they laughed and cried at the same time.

A Lock up on Crete

'Oh Tia you look amazing. It must be all this beautiful Cretan air,' Mel replied as she held out her hand to acknowledge Andreas.

'New Zealand is looking good on you too, Mel. We've hardly changed. Oh and you too Zoe,' Tia gushed as she realised a VIP was missing. 'Where's mitera sou?'

'My mother says 'hi' to you all. She's in the process of moving house nearer to me so she says she will see you next time. Mel's already seen her when she dropped us off at the airport.' Zoe explained.

'Ahhh that's nice. Give her my love when you return,' Tia added as they walked across to the car park.

Andreas drove them from the airport as the sun departed for the day and the three women babbled on about whereabouts they were up to in life.

'Zoe, as we are passing on the national road, shall I pull off where your little house is and we can show Mel?' asked Andreas as he switched on the car lights as they approached a tunnel.

'Yes that would make sense. It's the turning just after the windmill.' Zoe confirmed.

Andreas parked the car opposite the larger of the two village churches as Zoe led them through the tiny alleys, making sure she was going the right way in the fading light.

'I've had the roof replaced,' Zoe explained as she pointed up to the new concrete base. 'I want it to be a nice roof terrace with some shade,' she added as she led them inside.

A Lock up on Crete

'Wow, it's much bigger inside than I imagined,' Andreas began as the three women agreed.

After a little mooching around discussing which room could be renovated into a kitchen, bathroom and bedroom, Zoe locked the door and placed the key under a large stone as Andreas wondered just how many pairs of eyes, although there had been nobody around, had watched the four of them come and go.

They carried on their journey until Andreas pulled into a parking bay on the promenade in Agios Nikolaos. 'Why are we stopping here?' Zoe asked as Mel took in the sights and sounds of the nearby holidaymakers as they strolled along in the balmy August night air and reminisced about her time here with Bill. Happy memories flooded back. She chuckled when she remembered riding pillion on his battered moped and the way she had purposely thrust her chest into the small of his back whenever he braked. Oh to be back to that time, she thought.

'We are showing you your new lodgings for next week after you've outstayed your welcome in Iraepetra,' Tia explained with a smile and a wink.

They piled out of the car and followed Andreas up a few stone steps adorned with plant pots bursting with vivid colour. On the fourth step, Tia pulled a key from her bag and opened the bright blue door.

'Oh wow! I know where we are,' Zoe exclaimed as Andreas flicked on the electric and they followed him inside. Tia opened the balcony doors as the warm air

A Lock up on Crete

swept in and the magnificence of Mirabello Bay took their breath away.

'Welcome to my late uncle Manolis' little lock up. It is yours for next week after you have played havoc in Iraepetra.' Andreas's shoulders shook up and down as he chuckled remembering the three of them first arriving in Iraepetra as young women. What an impact they had made between them!

Tia produced a chilled bottle of Retsina and three glasses from the fridge. She gave one to Tia and the other to Zoe. Andreas took a little swig of his Raki from his hip flask.

'Yammas,' they cheered. 'Happy Reunion!'

'There's just one more thing to do now we are all reunited,' Zoe added as she carefully opened a letter that had arrived thirty years ago to her mother's address.

'Ok so remember the Cara mystery girls?' Zoe announced as she placed the aged blue air mail letter down on the table. 'This is a letter from Cara, a few months after she left us for the man from Milan. My mother had clean forgotten all about it arriving at her address until the other day when she was rummaging around in her box of memorabilia in the attic.'

The three reunited friends hunched in closer as Zoe read Cara's words written 32 years previously.

A Lock up on Crete

May 1985 Milan

Dear Zoe, Tia and Mel,
By now you have probably found my passport or rather
my cousin's passport I stupidly left behind. I have sent a
letter to the poste restante in Iraepetra but as yet have
not received a reply from you. So I thought I would send
one too to the only other address I have, which is Zoe's
home address in England.
So here goes – Zoe I can only imagine the confusion and
shock when and if you discovered my passport with my
photo but the same name as you – Zoe Matthews
Firstly, I was not trying to steal your identity. Zoe
Matthews is my cousin back in England. We were born
on the same day and our mothers decided that we would
both have one name the same as each other – me being
Cara Zoe Matthews and my cousin Zoe Cara Matthews.
We both look identical too and were like twins growing
up. My mother even made us the same home-made
clothes, much to the annoyance of Zoe as she did think
she was superior and in no need for home-made clothes.
* Anyway, as I divulged to you Tia, my folks were very*
poor and sadly died a few years before I met you all in
Guernsey. Zoe's parents were rich and lived in luxury
outside of Bristol. Thus, when I was desperate to meet
you again and travel to Crete, I went to stay with my
aunt and uncle for a week. My cousin Zoe was away at
the time and I was sleeping in her bed when I found her
'one year' passport. It was just so easy. I took it to a Loan
Shark and applied for a small loan which would set me

A Lock up on Crete

free on the road to Crete. I knew it was wrong but I was lonely and desperate to travel again. My aunt and uncle had no idea what I was up to and to this day have never questioned me about the loan or the missing one year passport - even my cousin Zoe! I did amend my ways though. You see, unbeknown to me, my man from Milan and my new husband was quite wealthy. He had listened to my guilty story and after we had assumed how much the greedy loan shark would have been demanding from my cousin, he wrote out a cheque and I posted it to my cousin in Bristol. I am yet to receive an acknowledgement from her although the cheque was cashed. Sadly and understandably so, they must have disowned me.
I hope you can forgive me, especially you Zoe! I thought the least I could do was to write to you all and explain why I had the same name as Zoe on my passport. I remembered it as we left Athens but I had my original passport I used to cross the border.
So that's it really - just an uncanny coincidence that we shared most of the same name, Zoe!
I really hope you girls are all well and I thank you again for taking me under your wing in Iraepetra. At least no one can take our memories away.
Please keep in touch.
Cara Zoe Matthews
xx

Andreas spoke as the three friends held each other's hands.

A Lock up on Crete

'So now all the mysteries have been solved: The mystery of the locket; the mystery of Cara Zoe Matthews and the mystery of the fate of Damianos.

'The only mystery now is - how are we going to persuade Mel to come and join us more often here in this blessed land of myths and legends?'

'I am so happy the three of you are finally reunited. And as us Cretans say: 'Etsi ine zoi' – such is life!'

THE END

Please if you can leave a review I would be very grateful. I hope you have enjoyed reading my novel and if you have never visited Crete and are able to do so, please GO! It's simply amazing.
Thank you
Elise

A Lock up on Crete

A Lock up on Crete

A Lock up on Crete

Printed in Great Britain
by Amazon